THE CHURCH
OF MY FATHER

ISBN 978-1-913218-51-5

Printed in Great Britain by
Biddles Books Limited, King's Lynn, Norfolk

CONTENTS

In memory of my father, Wilfrid, a true
Church of England clergyman

INTRODUCTION

My life I suppose has been a somewhat unbalanced one. It started conventionally enough in a middle-class household. I was sent to the local public school. In the 1960s and early 1970s it was a very old-fashioned establishment with the time-honoured pastimes of bullying and fagging to make men of especially the feebler boys of whom I was one. I was a reasonably bright boy academically and I was expected to achieve a good career. This I did not as, when I was about 17, I discovered the joys of alcohol and became rapidly addicted. This did not stop me going to university and attaining a reasonably good degree. But my further professional progress towards an intended legal career was thwarted both by drink and the second aspect of my personality problems known as bi-polar disorder. The combination of drink and bi-polarity finished my professional career prospects. I was able to obtain legally-related work which I did well for a long time but, towards the end of my 30s, I suffered further and more extreme bi-polar attacks. Again these, together with my continued heavy drinking, brought me low and in 2003 I suffered a quite severe car accident following a drinking binge. This finally brought me to my senses and I gave up drinking entirely after well over 25 years of over-indulgence. I had my bi-polar condition diagnosed and was prescribed the right medication to keep my moods stable.

But I was now in my mid-forties and the prospects of worthwhile employment were not good. I did some driving jobs for which I was not really suited. I also did some voluntary work. But in 2015 my wife and I moved to Sussex.

My real love had always been history and not law. I decided to offer history talks to groups and societies. I started with local societies and I now speak to organisations throughout the south-east of England.

I enjoyed writing the talks and so I thought I might write a book. But what to write about? Then, I thought about the Church. This was something that I had been brought up with, but which had not been a significant part of my life since I left home. Although I did not consider myself a deeply religious man, I did start going to Church again in about 2011. What better subject could there be than to write a history of the English Church from earliest times to the present day? But then I thought again, wouldn't this be deadly dull?

My late father was an eccentric traditional Church of England clergyman. So, why not tell the story through his eyes? This the book does, telling the story in his own mischievous and tongue-in-cheek style. Father was a man who seemed to get involved in scrapes and escapades and I have recounted these throughout the book to hopefully enhance its humour and charm. I have divided the book into monthly chapters. This is intended to follow the monthly newsletters of parish magazines. They are far too long to be those, but perhaps imagine a retired parish clergyman sitting back and deciding to write a series of essays for the benefit of his all too stupid former parishioners.

The story of the Roman Catholic Church is told from Roman times through the Dark Ages, the Anglo-Saxon era and from the Norman invasion in 1066 until the break with Rome in the early 1530s. It then tells the story of the Church of England to the present day. It particularly emphasises my father's time in the parish of Chigwell in the second half of the 20th century. Whilst it was hardly an area of great social need, it was typical of middle-class parishes of the time which remained vibrant until some way into the 1960s. Parish life is described during that era until it all began to fall apart under the pressure of the rebellion against authority, then known as the 'establishment', which took place at that time.

In my view it was these changes in attitudes that caused congregations to tail-off alarmingly from the 1960s onwards. But the Church of England identified the traditional liturgy as the principal culprit and set about replacing it with new forms of service. My father christened the Church authorities 'fools' for not recognising their very clear mistake. I can hear him now pacing about his study as he read the latest Diocesan directive 'fools, fools, fools' he would say. His terminology is used throughout the book to denote the people who run the Church of England now. A 'fool' is an ordained person of liberal, politically correct views who thinks that they are right about absolutely everything, but know next to nothing. In my view, this applies to most clergy today.

This book does have a serious message about the future of the Church of England. In my 'epilogue' I outline what I see as the state of the Anglican Church since my father's death. I seek a partial restoration of the old liturgy. I cannot stress enough that I am only looking for a partial restoration, as I recognise fully that the modern services must predominate given that there are now so many people for whom a traditional service would be alien. But Common Worship 2000 is a total Anglican resource book. Surely there must be room for traditional liturgy at main Sunday morning services just once a month or perhaps twice where there is a fifth Sunday? I have also made other suggestions for how a vibrant parochial ministry for the 21st century might come about. At the end of this book there is an opportunity, for those interested, to join a new 'Anglican Restoration Campaign' to campaign for the ideas that I have outlined.

I have thoroughly enjoyed putting this book together. I think that, together with my history talks, it has helped to finally put behind me all the negative aspects of my life. I hope that any readers will enjoy the book, both its historical and humorous side, and that, if they are concerned about the Church of England today, it may make them think seriously about its future.

I must thank Mrs Gretel Wakeham, Lay Reader at Seal Chart, Sevenoaks, Kent for reviewing the script. The views I have expressed are entirely my own but Gretel helped me to appreciate more the Church's vital social work in this country and overseas. Both my father and I tended to dismiss it as the work of 'do-gooders' rather than as a true expression of Christian belief. Yes, it is essential provided it springs from belief in God and Jesus Christ. Otherwise such work can be done just as well by non-believers. I hope the epilogue now stresses the correct emphasis.

I must thank my wife, Sally, particularly for helping me to edit and proof-read the script. This has proved a fraught and frequently acrimonious exercise. Sally has often made invaluable suggestions as to what the text should or should not contain.

I would like to thank my brother and his wife, Peter and Celia Dickinson, for providing the photographs of my father in his ecclesiastical cope and those of my father and mother on their wedding day and on their 40th wedding anniversary.

In respect of the history of the English Church up to the break with Rome in the early 1530s I have largely relied on two sources:-

A History of the Church in England - J R H Moorman ISBN 0 7136 1346 7 Morehouse Publishing

Christianity in England from Roman Times to the Reformation Vols 1 and 2 by Kenneth Hylson-Smith is © Kenneth Hylson-Smith, 1999. Published by SCM Press. rights@hymnsam.co.uk.

Extracts from the 'Good News Bible' are reproduced courtesy of

Good News Bible © 1994 published by the Bible Societies/HarperCollins Publishers Ltd,

Good News Bible © American Bible Society, 1966, 1971, 1976, 1992.

James Dickinson
Herstmonceux
East Sussex
September 2019

JANUARY

THE CHURCH FROM EARLIEST TIMES

Roman Christianity

The 1ˢᵗ Century Roman Empire stretched from the Middle East, including Palestine, through continental Europe to the Iberian Peninsula and the British Isles in the west. For the first 300 years Christianity was illegal. Under Roman law Christians were regarded as guilty of high treason and were liable to be executed. Their refusal, both to worship the emperor as a god and also to worship other pagan state gods, was seen as an incitement to riot. Early Christians participated in what was seen as threatening and unlawful assembly by gathering together secretly and late at night. Their religion was also seen as a form of magic unauthorised by law. To Christians, what was being asked of them, was a clear breach of the First Commandment, as handed down to Moses in the Book of Exodus: 'Thou shalt have no other gods but me'.

Whilst Christianity in Britain during Roman times was always a minority religion, Christians were to be found here from the late 2ⁿᵈ century onwards. The religion was not brought to Britain by missionaries and evangelism. It came about in a much more haphazard way, for example, through the influence of merchants and traders. Tertullian, a prolific early Christian author, wrote in about 200AD that 'parts of the Britains inaccessible to the Romans were indeed conquered by Christ'. These words, particularly, may have a bearing on the origins of Celtic Christianity in Britain. Celtic Christianity was essentially the same religion as that of

Roman Britain and Roman Gaul, but was preached against an unromanised and tribal background. But Christianity was able to offer so much more than paganism; it was open to all and salvation was a gift available for everyone.

Christianity remained illegal until the Emperor Constantine issued the Edict of Milan in 313. Until that point Christians were persecuted and punished for their faith throughout the empire including Britain. Most of us know of the tales of Christians being fed to the lions in ancient times in Rome. The practice was known as *damnatio ad bestias*. Nero had introduced a version of it in 64AD when Christians were convicted and put to death with dreadful cruelty. Some were covered with the skins of wild beasts and left to be eaten by dogs. Others were crucified. Many were burned alive and set on fire to serve as torches at night. However, the only contemporary reference to Christians being thrown to lions is in the texts of the Christian writer, Tertullian. He states that the ordinary public blamed Christians for any general misfortune and, after natural disasters, would cry 'Away with them to the lions!'. Tertullian also wrote that Christians started to avoid theatres and circuses which were associated with the place of their torture. In the 3rd century systematic persecution of Christians occurred under the Emperor Decius. Each man was required to testify before special commissioners that he had sacrificed to the gods and had shown reverence for the emperor's numen, that is, his divine power. True Christians at this time would not move from their beliefs and worship additional gods. In Roman Britain Christians were persecuted, tortured and martyred much as elsewhere although there is no evidence as such of *damnatio ad bestias*.

THE GREAT CHARIOT RACE
AGAINST TIME

In Roman times charioteering was undoubtedly a great sport amongst Romans. There was one occasion, where my father, almost chariot-like, broke the speed limit, undoubtedly in the service of the Lord! It was not in a vehicle built for speed, but that did not deter the great man where necessary. It was a Thursday and Ascension Day. Father took myself and my younger brother to Southend on Sea for the afternoon. We all had a lovely afternoon doing the usual Southend things walking up the pier and, in those days, getting the pier train back down. When we returned to the car to come home my father's faithful Morris Oxford turned out to have betrayed him and would not start. What was he to do? Not only did he need to get home with myself and Andrew he had the Ascension Day service to take that evening. The garage or AA man, I am not sure which, said there was nothing that could be done that day. Father was sent to a place where he might hire a vehicle. The only vehicle available was a large van with the logo 'Budget Rent A Van' emblazoned on both its sides. Goodness knows how much it cost to hire! Whether it was wangled on to parish expenses I have no idea! But so it was that father loaded us into this great machine and drove back to Chigwell down the A127, the Southend Arterial Road, like King Jehu from the Book of Kings in the Old Testament, riding furiously in his chariot over the body of Jezebel. It was to the amazement of my mother, on our return home, when he parked outside the vicarage in this giant, gaudy-painted, creature. All was saved though thanks to 'Budget Rent A Van' and father was there on time that evening to take the Ascension Day Service. What alternative did he have I could imagine him saying? Whether he told this story in his Ascension Day sermon that evening I do not remember. Knowing my father, he almost certainly did!

The story of St Alban

One great story of martyrdom in Roman Britain is that of St Alban, as told by the Venerable Bede, the great Anglo-Saxon monk, chronicler and historian. Bede said that, from the time of the martyrdom to his own day in the early 8th century, acts of healing and other miracles had not ceased at St Alban's tomb. The story of Alban is that, although not a Christian, he sheltered a priest fleeing from his persecutors. As a result of observing closely the vigils and prayers of the priest he decided to accept the Christian faith. The authorities became aware that a Christian was hiding in Alban's home. When soldiers arrived at his house Alban put on the priest's cloak and offered himself to them in the priest's place. He was brought before a judge who was conducting pagan rituals. He declared himself to be a Christian and, when he refused to recant, he was tortured and his execution ordered.

Alban was led to execution and he soon came to a fast-flowing river that could not be crossed, believed to be the River Ver. There was a bridge, but a mob of curious townspeople, who wished to watch the execution, had so clogged the bridge that the execution party could not cross. Alban wished to meet his maker quickly, so he raised his eyes to heaven and the river dried up, allowing Alban and his captors to cross over on dry land. The astonished executioner cast down his sword and fell at Alban's feet, moved by divine inspiration and praying that he might suffer either with Alban or be executed for him. The other executioners hesitated to pick up his sword, but went on about 500 paces with Alban to a gently sloping hill, covered completely with all kinds of wild flowers, and overlooking a beautiful plain (Bede observes that it was a fittingly beautiful place to be enriched and sanctified by a martyr's blood).

When Alban reached the summit of the hill he began to thirst and prayed God would give him water. A spring sprang up immediately at his feet. It was there that his head was struck off, as well as that of the first Roman soldier, who had refused to execute him and had then converted miraculously to the Christian faith. However, immediately after delivering the fatal stroke, the eyes of the new executioner popped out of his head and dropped to the ground, so that he could not rejoice over Alban's death. In later legends, Alban's head rolled downhill after his execution and a well sprang up where it stopped. Upon hearing of the miracle, the astonished judge ordered further persecutions to cease and he began to honour the saint's death.

St Alban's Cathedral now stands near the believed site of his execution and there is a well at the bottom of the hill known as Holywell Hill. The precise date of Alban's death is not known but the latest date given is 304AD which is the same as that of two other early British Christian martyrs, St Aaron and St Julius.

The story of Alban's death is a great tale of early Christian courage and belief. It is one of the most powerful stories of

Christian martyrdom both in Britain and elsewhere. How many of us would be prepared to die for the Christian faith as Alban did?

The continued spread of the early Church

Constantine decided to decriminalise Christianity in 313AD by the Edict of Milan. This was clearly a turning point for early Christianity, sometimes referred to as the Triumph of the Church, the Peace of the Church or the Constantinian Shift. Christianity was raised to a new standard as the Emperor's 'first and principal concern'. The Edict of Thessalonica, issued on 27 February 380AD, by three reigning Roman Emperors, ordered all subjects of the Roman Empire to profess the faith of the bishops of Rome and of Alexandria, making Nicene Christianity the state religion of the Roman Empire.

Once Christianity was no longer illegal, churches and chapels were built and rebuilt, feast days were celebrated and holy ceremonies were carried out. Following the end of religious persecution British bishops were able to attend the Council of Arles in 314. Those present were the Bishops of the City of York, the City of London and the City of Lincoln. They were accompanied by other priests and deacons. This showed that the normal church ranks applied in Britain as elsewhere and that the church in Britain was now sufficiently significant to be invited to as important a Church Council as that at Arles. The Council adopted 22 canons on Church life across Britain, Gaul, Italy, Spain, Germany and Africa. Rome was acknowledged as the supreme authority of the Church and it was also proclaimed that the date of Easter should be celebrated on one day throughout the world.

In the 4th century St Martin of Tours (316-397AD) had a remarkable impact on church life both in Gaul and in

Britain. After many years as a soldier he became a hermit, but then, bowing to the overwhelming and persistent pressure of the people, he became Bishop of Tours. He established monasticism and carried out a vigorous brand of evangelism throughout his diocese. Martin visited Britain in 396AD and the nature of his evangelism inspired British Christians at the time. He also inspired the lives of St Ninian, St Patrick and St Columba in the following two centuries which had such an impact on the spiritual life of the church in Ireland and Scotland and from there to the north of England.

Christianity was not an organised religion publicly until the 4th century. It was not until the second decade that the church in Britain was organised as in other western provinces of the empire. Groups of Christians would meet, either in their own homes or sometimes in purpose-built churches, directed by the clerical hierarchy of bishops, priests and deacons. This hierarchy reflects that still used today.

Christian worship, as set out in the earliest 2nd century texts of Didache, Ignatius of Antioch and Justin Martyr, was principally a eucharistic one on a Sunday. It was only the baptised who were admitted to what became known as the 'mass' of which there was no set pattern other than that described by Justin Martyr. Adult rather than infant baptism was a sacrament of central importance to the church. Those seeking to become Christians started as *catechumens,* that is, persons receiving instruction in preparation for Christian baptism. Baptism was the crucial rite of passage for those seeking membership of their local church. It would have taken place during one of the major church feasts such as Easter or Pentecost.

By the mid-3rd century Christians had an established form of creed which may have originated in the 2nd century:-

I believe in God the Father Almighty; and in Jesus Christ His only Son our Lord, who was born of the Holy Ghost and the Virgin Mary, who was crucified under Pontius Pilate and buried, rose again the third day from the dead, ascended into heaven, sits on the right hand of the Father, whence he will come to judge the living and dead; and in the Holy Ghost, the Holy Church, the remission of sins, the resurrection of the flesh.

This wording clearly foreshadows that of the Apostles' Creed which reflects still the heart of our faith today. In its traditional form the wording in the Anglican Church is as follows:-

I believe in God the Father Almighty, Maker of heaven and earth.

And in Jesus Christ His only son our Lord; who was conceived by the Holy Ghost, born of the Virgin Mary, suffered under Pontius Pilate, was crucified, dead, and buried; he descended into hell; the third day he rose again from the dead; he ascended into heaven, and sitteth on the right hand of God the Father Almighty; from thence he shall come to judge the quick and the dead.

I believe in the Holy Ghost; the holy catholic Church; the communion of saints; the forgiveness of sins; the resurrection of the body; and the life everlasting.

Amen.

During the late Roman period the other major creed in use by the Christian church was developed. This is the Nicene Creed, originally adopted in the city of Nicaea by the First Council of Nicaea in 325AD. It has been an integral part of the worship of the Roman Catholic Church from earliest times and remains also a central part of Anglican Church worship to this day:-

We believe in one God,
the Father, the Almighty,
maker of heaven and earth,
of all that is, seen and unseen.

We believe in one Lord, Jesus Christ,
the only Son of God,
eternally begotten of the Father,
God from God, Light from Light,
true God from true God,
begotten, not made,
of one Being with the Father.
Through him all things were made.

For us and for our salvation
he came down from heaven:
by the power of the Holy Spirit
he became incarnate from the Virgin Mary,
and was made man.

For our sake he was crucified under Pontius Pilate;
he suffered death and was buried.
On the third day he rose again
in accordance with the Scriptures;
he ascended into heaven
and is seated at the right hand of the Father.
He will come again in glory to judge the living and the dead,
and his kingdom will have no end.

We believe in the Holy Spirit, the Lord, the giver of life,
who proceeds from the Father and the Son.
With the Father and the Son he is worshipped and glorified.
He has spoken through the Prophets.
We believe in one holy catholic and apostolic Church.
We acknowledge one baptism for the forgiveness of sins.
We look for the resurrection of the dead,
and the life of the world to come.

Amen.

After the Romans departed from Britain in 410AD their influence remained. Christianity did not suddenly come to an end. When Germanus, the Bishop of Auxerre and evangelist, came to England in 429AD and 435/6AD he encountered groups of Christians in considerable numbers. When Augustine arrived in 597AD he found a British church with its own bishops. Indeed, Augustine's mission was as much an act of restoration as of conversion.

Post-Roman Christianity from 410AD to 597AD

Roman occupation of Britain ended in about 410AD but Saint Augustine of Canterbury's mission to restore Roman Christianity to these islands did not begin until 597AD. There is very little known about the years in between; a period which has come to be known as 'The Dark Ages'. *Maybe this is not too dissimilar from the one we are living through today, both secular and ecclesiastical.* But Christianity did survive, predominately in the form of 'Celtic' Christianity.

While Roman Christianity fitted itself into the framework of the Roman empire's imperial institutions, 'Celtic' Christianity had grown up against the tribal background of the peoples who followed it. So, there were some differences of practice between the two traditions. The most noteworthy being the means of determining the date of Easter. Owing to its relative isolation from the rest of Western Christendom, the Celtic Church did not adopt the various alterations which, on astronomical rather than theological grounds, had been accepted by the Roman Church.

The second difference was the monastical method of shaving the head; the tonsure. The Roman tonsure was formed by the top of the head being shaved close and a circle or crown of hair left to grow around it. The Celtic tonsure, also known as the transverse tonsure, consisted in shaving all the hair in front of a line drawn over the top of the head from ear to ear.

So, the differences between Celtic and Roman Christianity were never more than skin-deep — *perhaps no more important than the shape and cut of a tonsure. But, given the nature of the human rather than divine condition, the two issues of the date of Easter and the tonsure became a matter of the utmost significance to the two churches, leading in Saxon times to the Synod of Whitby in 664 AD when the Roman tradition triumphed.*

However, it is not by examining differences in church practice, but by looking at the lives of the great Christian men of the Post-Roman period that we obtain the most vivid impression of its history. So, I will now tell you about these people. Most of you will have heard of St Patrick and I will start with him. The others are also great men of the early church although not much remembered today, apart from St David. It is about time that their deeds and exploits were recalled.

THE GIANTS OF THE EARLY CHURCH

When my father was Vicar of Chigwell there were two great giants of the local church. He was, of course, the first and the second was the chaplain of Chigwell School. Effectively they were professional rivals and disliked one another intensely. Daggers drawn, if not openly, then certainly in a covert manner. Father was a broad-church Anglican. The chaplain was a fiery, Welsh, intellectual, High Church Anglo-Catholic and an extraordinarily fine English teacher. They lived virtually on top of one another. The vicarage garden overlooked that of the school house, 'Harsnetts', where the chaplain and his family lived. I suppose that you can say that my father and the chaplain fought a kind of turf war. I did not help matters myself when I took an old wooden door, blocking a derelict outhouse building, which the chaplain had put there to prevent his dalmatian dogs getting through to the vicarage garden, and used it for our annual November 5th bonfire! How was I to know that such an apparently useless piece of wood was so essential? Anyway, the chaplain certainly tore me off a strip of which he was more than capable of doing. I am sure my father and the chaplain had more fundamental grounds for their dislike; churchmanship, mainly, I suspect! But father and the chaplain did make it up in the end because they both had to deal with a neurotic and half-mad musician from Yorkshire who both was the church organist and the school's music teacher. This man was prone to making threats of suicide and sought the soothing balm of both father and the chaplain to deal with his latest nervous breakdown. I do not know what father and the chaplain exactly did. Perhaps they applied some ecumenical Anglican/Anglo-Catholic healing lotion both to the organist and their own relationship. But Herod and Pilate did indeed become friends. I seem to remember that the chaplain and his wife invited my parents to spend a night with them at their home in mid- Wales. I understand that this was not a total success, so perhaps the wars of religion broke out again! But such were the lives of the true prophets of the early church.

St Patrick

By far the most famous saint of this period is St Patrick. Most people know him as the patron saint of Ireland and many celebrate St Patrick's Day on 17th March. But Patrick was not Irish. He was born near Bristol in about 385AD. His father was a gentleman and a Christian deacon who owned a small estate in a place called *Bannavem Taburniae*. Although scholars are not sure exactly where this place was, it was probably on the west coast around Bristol, near the southern border of modern Wales and England. But Patrick was not an active Christian initially. The Confession of St Patrick says that, at the age of sixteen, he was captured by a group of Irish pirates. They took him to Ireland where he was enslaved and held captive for six years. While in captivity he worked as a shepherd, which strengthened his relationship with God through prayer, enabling him to convert to Christianity.

After six years of captivity Patrick heard a voice telling him that he would soon go home. Patrick escaped and fled to a port on Ireland's east coast. He boarded a ship bound for Britain. The captain, a pagan, did not like the look of him and demanded that Patrick 'suck his breasts,' a ritual gesture symbolising acceptance of the captain's authority. *It sounds somewhat unappealing to me and Patrick, indeed, refused.* Instead he tried to convert the crew. For some reason, the captain still took him aboard. After three days' sailing, the ship landed in England and Patrick then returned home to his family, now a young man in his early twenties.

A few years after returning home Patrick had a vision requesting him to go back to Ireland to minister, in the name of Jesus Christ, to the people there. Before returning Patrick studied in Europe, mainly at Auxerre, and became a monk. Subsequently he was ordained to the priesthood. Patrick was consecrated later a bishop and went back to Ireland in 432AD.

After Patrick's evangelical mission started serious allegations were made against him by his fellow Christians. It was alleged that he was bribed by wealthy women bearing lavish gifts. Patrick says that these were returned always. He denied also accepting illicit payments for carrying out baptisms and for ordaining priests. This alleged financial impropriety may have extended to the way in which his bishopric in Ireland was secured. There may also have been allegations of a sordid nature about Patrick's private life to which he replied 'They brought up against me after thirty years something I had already confessed ... some things I had done one day - rather, in one hour, when I was young'. Patrick does not tell us what he did exactly; worship idols or perhaps engage in forbidden sexual practices? Whatever it was, Patrick understood his Irish mission to be penance for his youthful sins. While he spread Christianity around Ireland, he was often beaten, put in chains or made subject to extortion. 'Every day there is the chance that I will be killed, or surrounded, or taken into slavery'.

We can see clearly from the nature of Patrick's mission how, due to the work of mischief-makers, some of the allegations came to be made against him. Whilst he writes that he 'baptised thousands of people' he also states that he ordained priests to lead the new Christian communities, that he converted wealthy women and that he also dealt with the sons of kings converting them too.

Two centuries after his death, Irish believers desired rather more exciting stories of Patrick's life than the saint's own account. One legend, written about 700AD, describes Patrick's contest with native religious leaders, the druids. The druids insulted Patrick, tried to poison him and engaged him in magical duels in which they competed to manipulate the weather, destroy each other's sacred books and survive raging fires. When one druid dared to take the name of the Lord God in vain Patrick sent the druid flying into the air. The man dropped to the ground and broke his skull. *This served the blaspheming druid entirely right, I should say.*

Another legend relates to Patrick's evangelising journey back to Ireland from his parents' home near Bristol. He is understood to have carried with him an ash-wood walking stick or staff. He thrust this stick into the ground wherever he was evangelising. At the place now known as Aspatria, meaning Ash of Patrick, his message took so long to get through to the people there that the stick had taken root by the time he was ready to move on. *Perhaps Patrick had gone on talking too long and sent his congregation to sleep, something of which I have known all too well in my experience of preachers, other than myself of course.*

Whilst Patrick became finally the Bishop of Armagh the diocesan system in Ireland failed largely given the lack of any real cities to sustain it. Instead it was the monasteries which Patrick founded that became the chief feature of the Irish Church. Patrick was a great evangelist who spread Christianity the length and breadth of Ireland and is, without doubt, one of the great heroes of the early church in these islands.

St Columba

Columba was born in Donegal in the north of Ireland in about 521AD. When he attained sufficient literary skills he entered the monastic school of Movilla at Newtownards under St Finian, a man noted for his sanctity and learning, who had studied at the *Magnum Monasterium* of St Ninian on the shores of Galloway. At about the age of twenty and, ordained a deacon, he travelled southwards into Leinster. Columba later entered the monastery of Clonard, which was governed at that time also by Finian himself. Here he drank in the traditions of the Welsh Church since Finian had been trained in the learning of St David. The average number of students at Clonard was about 3,000. Columba was one of the twelve students of St Finian who became known as the Twelve Apostles of Ireland. He became a monk and eventually was ordained a priest. Columba was a striking figure, of great stature and powerful build, with a loud, melodious voice which, it was said, could be heard from one hilltop to another.

The name Columba means 'dove', but, in nature, the saint was anything but that. In or around 560AD, Columba became involved in a quarrel with Finian over a psalter. He is said to have copied this at the scriptorium under Finian intending to keep the copy. Finian disputed his right to keep the copy. *Perhaps this was the first ever copyright dispute.* The dispute eventually led to the pitched Battle of Cul Dreimhne, in what is now County Sligo, in 561AD, during which many men were killed. *This was an appalling outcome for a dispute over a mere written text. Certainly, one can now understand the expression: 'Men have died for less'.* A synod of clerics and scholars threatened to excommunicate him for these deaths, but St. Brendan of Birr spoke on his behalf as a result of which he was allowed to go into exile instead. Columba had a guilty conscience about what had happened and he decided to atone for his sins by going into exile and winning for Christ as many souls as had perished in the terrible battle of Cul Dreimhne. He left Ireland, to return only once, many years later.

In 563AD Columba travelled to Scotland with twelve companions in a wicker currach covered with leather. According to legend he first landed on the Kintyre Peninsula, near Southend. *Not the one in my beloved Essex where I was married.* However, being still in sight of his native land, he moved further north up the west coast of Scotland. The island of Iona was made over to him by his kinsman Conall mac Comgaill, King of Dal Riata, who had perhaps invited him to come to Scotland in the first place. Iona provided thus the only centre of literacy in the region. His reputation as a holy man led to his role as a diplomat among the tribes. *Clearly the quality of his diplomatic work in Ireland had not preceded him.*

There are also many stories of miracles which he performed during his work to convert the Picts, the most famous being his encounter with an unidentified animal that some have equated with the Loch Ness Monster. It is said that he banished a ferocious 'water beast', *undoubtedly called Nessie,* to the depths of the River Ness, after it had killed a Pict and then tried to attack Columba's disciple named Lugne. *The mystery is solved. The Scottish tourist industry will die now. Truth will out. If only people had read about Columba properly in the first place this daft Loch Ness monster story would never have taken hold.* Columba visited the pagan King Bridei, King of Fortriu, at his base in Inverness, winning Bridei's respect, although not his conversion. He founded a new abbey as a base for spreading Christianity among the northern Pictish kingdoms. The abbey became a centre for literacy in the region. He played subsequently a major role in the politics of the country. He was also very energetic in his work as a missionary, and, in addition to founding several churches in the Hebrides, he worked to turn his monastery at Iona into a school for missionaries. He was a renowned man of letters, having written several hymns and being credited with having transcribed 300 books. One of the few times he left Scotland was towards the end of his life, when he returned to Ireland to found the monastery of Durrow.

Columba died on Iona and was buried in 597AD by his monks in the abbey he had created. In 794AD the Vikings descended on Iona. Columba's remains were finally removed in 849AD and divided between Scotland and Ireland. He is the patron saint of Derry.

St Germanus

Germanus, Bishop of Auxerre, was sent to England in 429AD, not as a missionary, but to stamp out what is called the Pelagian heresy. This shows that there must have been a large number of English Christians at the time for his visit to have been necessary. Germanus had been previously a professional soldier and was a man of great bravery and strength of character. He found the English Celts to be a particularly timid lot and trained them as a fighting force to take on a marauding army of Picts and Scots near Mold in Flintshire. As the enemy forces advanced Germanus ordered his men to repeat his battle-cry in one great shout. The bishops shouted 'Alleluia' three times and all the army replied in unison with a mighty roar of 'Alleluia', literally meaning 'Praise the Lord!', such that the enemy was overcome completely with fear and fled. The battle was won, without the shedding of blood, a victory brought about by faith and not by might. *It reminds me of my own Easter greeting to the Church Choir before the service when I said 'Christ is Risen' to which I expected a more than lusty response of 'Alleluia' and would repeat the invitation until I got the appropriate level of response.*

The Choir was not allowed to go afterwards until it had done so. No half-measures were to be allowed for the Queen of all Christian seasons.

St David

David, the patron saint of Wales, was born in about 500AD, reputedly on a cliff top near Capel Non (Non's chapel), on the South-West Wales coast during a fierce storm. Both his parents were descended from Welsh royalty. He was the son of Sandde, Prince of Powys, and Non, daughter of a chieftain of Menevia, now the little cathedral town of St David's.

The young David grew up to be a priest, being educated at the monastery of Hen Fynyw under the tutorage of St Paulinus. According to legend David performed several miracles during his life, including restoring Paulinus' sight. It is also said that, during a battle against the Saxons, David advised his soldiers to wear leeks in their hats so that they could be distinguished easily from their enemies, which is why the leek is now one of the emblems of Wales.

David was a vegetarian, who ate only bread, herbs and vegetables and who drank only water. David became known as Aquaticus or Dewi Ddyfrwr (the water drinker) in Welsh. Sometimes, as a self-imposed penance, he would stand up to his neck in a lake of cold water, reciting scripture. *He must have thought he was very bad to have gone that far. I am afraid that I was always a man much too inclined to his creature comforts to have endured such torture, even for the Lord. But, then I am certainly no saint.* Springs of water were supposed to appear when important milestones in David's life occurred.

On becoming a missionary David travelled throughout Wales and Britain and made a pilgrimage to Jerusalem, where he was consecrated a bishop. He founded twelve monasteries, including Glastonbury and one at Minevia, which he made his episcopal seat. He was named Archbishop of Wales at the Synod of Brevi (Llandewi Brefi) in Cardiganshire in 550AD.

St David died on 1 March 589AD, at Minevia. Some maintain that he did not die until 601AD, which would have made him over 100 years old. His remains were buried in a shrine at St David's Cathedral, which was ransacked in the 11th century by Viking invaders, who plundered the site and murdered two Welsh bishops.

After his death, his influence spread far and wide, first throughout Britain and then to Brittany. In 1120, Pope Callactus II canonised David as a saint. Following this he was declared Patron Saint of Wales. Such was David's influence that many pilgrimages were made to St. David's and the Pope decreed that two pilgrimages made to St. David's equalled one to Rome while three were worth one to Jerusalem! Fifty churches in South Wales alone bear his name. Many of the true facts of David's life are unknown, but, like St Patrick, he was a great evangelist, in his case throughout Wales and the wider British Isles and a true hero of the early church.

Pelagius

Pelagius was born about 354-360AD. He is said to have been of British origin. He was tall in stature and portly in appearance. Pelagius was also highly educated, he spoke and wrote Latin and Greek with great fluency and was well versed in theology. Pelagius became well known around 380AD when he moved to Rome. There he enjoyed a reputation for austerity. Pelagius became concerned about the moral laxity of society. He blamed this laxity on the theology of divine grace preached by St Augustine of Hippo amongst others. He began to teach a very strict and rigid moralism; this emphasised a natural, innate human ability to attain salvation. When Alaric sacked Rome in 410AD, Pelagius fled to Carthage where he continued his work. By 415AD he was in Jerusalem. The view that mankind can avoid sinning and humans can choose freely to obey God's commandments, stands at the core of Pelagian teaching. Pelagius stressed human autonomy and freedom of the will.

For Pelagius the gift of grace consisted of free will, the Law of Moses and the teachings of Jesus. A person with this gift would be able to perceive the correct moral course of action and to follow it. Prayer, fasting, and asceticism supported the will to do good. Pelagius claimed that all good works were done only with the grace of God, which he saw as enabling, but not forcing, good works. He believed that infants must be baptised for salvation. He also thought that saints were not always sinless, but that they had the capacity to stop sinning.

Pelagius said, 'This grace we for our part do not, as you suppose, allow to consist merely in the law, but also in the help of God. God helps us by His teaching and revelation; He opens the eyes of our heart; He points out to us the future that we may not be absorbed in the present; He discovers to us the snares of the devil; He enlightens us with the manifold and ineffable gift of heavenly grace.' In a letter to the Pope defending himself, he stated, 'This free will is in all good works always assisted by divine help', and in an accompanying confession of faith, 'Free-will we do so own, as to say that we always stand in need of God's help', However, he affirmed that 'We do also abhor the blasphemy of those who say that any impossible thing is commanded to man by God; or that the commandments of God cannot be performed by any one man', a statement which the Pope approved of upon receiving the letter, whereas Augustine famously stated *'non possum non peccare'*: 'I cannot not sin'.

Pelagius was expelled from Jerusalem after the Roman Church condemned his views as heretical. He was allowed to settle in Egypt, but he was not heard from afterwards. Some continue to regard the views of Pelagius as heresy. The clash between free will and pre-destination has bedevilled the church down the centuries and, particularly, in the Roman Catholic Church remains an issue to this day.

———————————

Patrick, Columba, Germanus, David and Pelagius were all highly educated men. There must have been a strong continuing link between the Roman Church on the continent and these islands after the departure of the Romans themselves from our shores. Christianity did not die on the departure of the Romans.* On the contrary it continued to survive and, maybe even flourish, thanks, not least, to the efforts of these great men of the early church. *These men were as far as it is possible to get from the insipid and anodyne characters, lacking totally in genuine leadership qualities, who inhabit the episcopal bench of the Church of England today.*

———————————

* As borne out as recently as May 2019 when an apparently Christian Anglo-Saxon tomb was discovered at Prittlewell, Southend-on-Sea, dating from about 580AD.

CHRISTIANITY IN ANGLO-SAXON ENGLAND FROM 597AD TO THE END OF THE NINTH CENTURY

St Augustine's Mission to England in 597AD

In 596AD Pope Gregory the Great decided to send a full-scale mission to England to convert the largely pagan Anglo-Saxons to the Christian faith. Although he was the first Pope from a monastic background, he had prior political experience from his time in government before going into the Church, which may have helped him to be a talented administrator. He established successfully papal supremacy. During his papacy he improved greatly the welfare of the people of Rome. Throughout the Middle Ages he was known as 'the Father of Christian Worship' because of his exceptional efforts in revising the Roman worship of his day. His contributions to the development of the Divine Liturgy of the Pre-Sanctified Gifts, still in use in the Byzantine Rite, were so significant that he is recognised generally as its *de facto* author. Gregory is a Doctor of the Church and one of the Latin Fathers. He is considered a saint in the Catholic Church and the Eastern Orthodox Church. He is also honoured by the Anglican Church. The Protestant reformer John Calvin admired Gregory greatly and declared in his *Institutes* that Gregory was the last good Pope!

Legend has it that Gregory, before he became Pope, happened to see a group of Angle children from Deira, a

Celtic kingdom in northern England, awaiting sale as slaves in the Roman market or forum. The Anglo-Saxon monk and historian, Bede, says that Gregory was struck by the unusual appearance of the slaves and asked about their background. When they said they were 'Anglii' (Angles), he replied with a series of puns that 'It is well, for they have an angelic face, and such people ought to be co-heirs of the angels in heaven'. Then he asked who was the king of their people? They replied 'Aelli' to which Gregory responded 'Alleluia, God's praise must be heard there'. When asked the name of their tribe they answered 'Deire' to which Gregory responded 'They shall indeed be rescued *de ira,* that is from wrath, to the mercy of Christ'. Supposedly, this encounter inspired Gregory to launch a mission to bring Christianity to their countrymen in England. It was from the name 'Anglii' that the name 'England' is derived. This is clearly a lovely story but its precise truth cannot be known. *It is often said that this story is well known by most people, but of how many is this truly the case today?*

Whilst Gregory had undoubtedly a genuine interest in the spiritual and other welfare of the English there may have been other more hard-headed reasons at work. At that time the state of the Roman Church was somewhat shaky and its position in Gaul and Spain was weak. Gregory was successful in restoring the position of the Church in those two countries. Possibly he felt that a successful mission to England would both help the position of the Church in Gaul and Spain and bolster also the position of the entire Catholic Church as a whole.

Initially he wanted to lead the mission himself, but the Roman people themselves would not let him go since they saw him as the future head of the Church. On the death of Pope Pelagius in 590AD Gregory was chosen as his successor and was then able to start planning the mission to England. As part of this Gregory arranged in 595AD for English boys, aged seventeen to eighteen, to be bought in the slave markets of Marseilles and placed in continental monasteries with a view to them going on the mission to increase its chances of success.

Gregory chose as the leader of the expedition a man called Augustine. Augustine was the prior of St Andrew's monastery on the Coelian Hill. He led a party of 40 monks, including the English boys referred to previously, which left Rome in the summer of 596AD. It was not long afterwards that Augustine and his followers began to get cold feet. Bede states that 'they became afraid and began to consider returning home. For they were appalled at the idea of going to a barbarous, fierce and pagan nation of whose very language they were ignorant'. Augustine started to return home, but Gregory sent him back telling him in no uncertain terms to carry out his mission. Augustine was made an abbot to increase his authority among his followers and subsequently probably a bishop.

The party finally reached the channel coast. They took a ship northwards and sailed up the English south-eastern coast. They went down the River Stour towards the old Roman city of Durovernum, now Canterbury. Augustine decided not to go direct to the city but to send a message ahead to King Ethelbert of Kent saying that he had come from Rome to spread the Christian faith. Ethelbert was the most powerful Anglo-Saxon ruler of his day. Whilst Ethelbert was a pagan, his wife, Bertha, was already a Christian. She was a Frankish princess who had been determined to keep her Christian faith in the overwhelmingly pagan culture in which she now lived. She had been allowed to bring a bishop called Liudhard with her to Canterbury and they worshipped together at the Church of St Martin, dating from Roman times, outside the city walls. By the time Augustine arrived Ethelbert had known the company of Christians for more than a decade. It was most unlikely that Ethelbert was going to give the Christians a hostile reception. Pope Gregory had undoubtedly taken these factors into account when he planned the mission.

Augustine and his mission stayed initially on the Isle of Thanet. There they were visited by Ethelbert and his followers. The missionaries were allowed to preach about the Christian faith. Ethelbert did not accept the faith unconditionally, but he promised the mission party continued hospitality and said that they were at liberty to try to spread the Christian word by evangelism. The mission was granted somewhere to live in Canterbury itself. Its work continued and achieved great success. At some point, we do not know precisely when, Ethelbert was himself converted to the Christian faith and baptised. His conversion acted as an incentive to his subjects to embrace Christianity. Pope Gregory wrote to the Patriarch of Alexandria on Christmas Day 597AD that Augustine had baptised more than 10,000 converts to the faith. Augustine began now to extend his mission to other parts of Kent and maybe to other kingdoms. He was granted another residence in Canterbury, which was sufficiently large for part to be used as a church. He dedicated the church to 'Christ, the Holy Saviour' thus establishing Canterbury Cathedral as the church of his diocese. But it was only gradually that Augustine came to be accepted as the first Archbishop of Canterbury. He died in 604AD.

Augustine was really a very limited man; he hesitated on his way to England and, whilst he had undoubted success in converting many people in the south of England to

Christianity, he was very much assisted by the favourable conditions there. He antagonised his brother bishops of the Celtic tradition. Legend has it that the Celtic bishops obtained the advice of a much-respected recluse, before meeting Augustine, who said that if he rose to greet them then he and his opinions were deserving of respect. But if he failed to rise then he did not deserve respect. Augustine was an arrogant man who did not stand up and his opinions were ignored as a consequence. *I am not sure that his achievements merited him being made a saint by the early Church.*

CASTING PEARLS BEFORE SWINE

My father once preached a sermon about the great theologian, St Augustine of Hippo. As is usual I made one of my famed *faux pas*. I thought he was talking about Augustine of Canterbury. 'You stupid boy', or words to that effect, my father said! But how many of you know the difference between the great theologian and the minor missionary to England? Since I did not know I am sure that neither my sister nor two brothers would have done. Perhaps the standard of father's own religious instruction to his family was not entirely up to scratch. Perhaps, more likely, we were all, like the common herd, just pig ignorant!

The Synod of Whitby 664AD

For 60 years after Augustine's death in 604AD Christianity continued to spread throughout the British Isles by missionaries both of the Celtic and Roman traditions. Roman missionaries went both to East Anglia and the west of England. They also went to the north of England, but their work had to stop when pagan forces thwarted them and they had to flee. Subsequently their work was taken up by Celtic missionaries who were continuing already their missionary work in Ireland and Scotland. They spread the good news into north-eastern England and founded the great monastery at Lindisfarne.

Whilst, in practical terms, the differences between the two religious traditions were insubstantial reconciliation was necessary for the good of both. The Celtic Christians realised that, although they were far from being a minority in the British Isles, they were vastly smaller when compared to the continental Roman Catholic Church governed from Rome. The two traditions needed to come together to continue effectively their work in these islands. The Romans held effectively all the cards given their extensive and authoritative church system.

In 664AD King Oswy of Northumbria called a meeting of the two traditions, which came to be known as 'The Synod of Whitby'. Oswy was a Christian of the Celtic tradition, but his wife supported the Roman. The leader of the Roman delegation was Abbot Wilfrid of Ripon. Oswy called on Bishop Colman of Lindisfarne to outline the position of the Celtic Church. Wilfrid responded for the Romans. All that was at stake was the calculation of the date of Easter and the shape of clerical tonsures. *I never had to worry about the length of my hair since I started going bald at about the age of 18.*

The oratory of Wilfrid *(I am proud, rightly, of my own sermons, so perhaps I was inspired by my namesake)* won the day finally since he relied on St Peter as the foundation of the authority of the Roman Church. At the end he quoted St Matthew xvi vvs18-19: 'Thou art Peter; and upon this rock I will build my church; and the gates of hell shall not prevail against it. And I will give unto thee the keys of the kingdom of heaven'. Oswy then ruled in favour of the Roman Church. Afterwards, whilst there continued to be some disharmony, the Church developed gradually in line with the Roman tradition. But England was suffering from a period of considerable political instability and warfare between the various Anglo-Saxon kingdoms which hindered the progress of Church unity. This undermined the efforts of Christian leaders to spread the faith of our Lord. They were also hindered by widespread plague which claimed, in addition to large numbers of the general population, also the lives of the East Anglian bishop, Cedd, and that of the new prospective Archbishop of Canterbury, Wighard. The Church was unable to minister properly its word against such a background and many feared that it would fall apart. The Church was saved largely through the work of three men and was then able to prosper.

Archbishop Theodore of Tarsus

St Theodore of Tarsus was the first great Archbishop of Canterbury. He was appointed to the archiepiscopate in 668AD by Pope Vitalian at the age of 67. He was a Greek of the Byzantine tradition. The Pope saw him as the man of outstanding academic and practical ability to move the English Church forward. On his arrival in England in 669AD with Hadrian, a man who had turned down the archbishopric for himself, he toured the whole of England where he was welcomed universally.

Theodore realised that education was crucial to the further spread of Christianity. Theodore and Hadrian established a school in Canterbury, providing instruction in both Greek and Latin, resulting in a 'golden age' of Anglo-Saxon scholarship. The Venerable Bede said:

'They attracted a large number of students, into whose minds they poured the waters of wholesome knowledge day by day. In addition to instructing them in the Holy Scriptures, they also taught their pupils poetry, astronomy, and the calculation of the church calendar... Never had there been such happy times as these since the English settled in Britain'.

Theodore also taught sacred music, introduced various texts, knowledge of Eastern saints and may even have been responsible for the introduction of the Litany of the Saints, a major liturgical innovation. Some of his thoughts are accessible in the Biblical Commentaries and notes compiled by his students at the Canterbury School. Pupils from the school at Canterbury were sent out as Benedictine abbots in southern England, distributing the curriculum of Theodore.

When Theodore arrived, whilst Christianity was by then established in all but one of the Saxon kingdoms, its structure was extremely flimsy. There were only seven dioceses three of which were unoccupied. In the remaining four only two of the bishops had unquestionably been installed according to the rules of the Church. By the time of Theodore's death in 690AD there were thirteen to fourteen bishoprics whose incumbents had been appointed properly. Theodore's immediate successor added two or three more.

Theodore found confusion as to who were the appropriate bishops. He took decisive action. He made Chad Bishop of the Mercians with his diocesan seat at Lichfield. Eleutherius from Gaul was made Bishop of the West Saxons with his diocesan seat at Winchester and Wilfrid was made the Bishop of York. Theodore called a synod at Hertford to discuss the subdivision of these three very large dioceses. This policy was opposed by Wilfrid. Due to Wilfrid's obstructionism the issue was not settled at Hertford. But in time what Theodore wanted prevailed. When the Bishop of the East Saxons became too feeble to resist, his diocese was divided into two and in 678AD, when Wilfrid was exiled from Northumbria, his own diocese was divided into three and subsequently into five.

Unlike Augustine, Theodore had a charismatic personality, able to convince others of the need for change. He obtained agreement to ten new canons covering crucial issues such as marriage and divorce. He also intervened in secular matters, securing peace in areas divided by war between the kings themselves. This led to greater political stability in which the Church could flourish. The Venerable Bede said that 'never had there been such happy times....for having such brave Christian kings, they were a terror to all the barbarian nations, and desires of all men were set on the joys of the heavenly kingdom of which they had only lately heard; while all who wished for instruction in sacred studies had teachers ready to hand'. This was Theodore's magnificent achievement. Theodore died in 690AD at the age of 88, having held the archbishopric for twenty-two years. He was buried in Canterbury at the church known today as St Augustine's Abbey. He is regarded as a saint in the Roman Catholic, Anglican and Eastern Orthodox Churches.

St Wilfrid

Wilfrid was a giant of the Anglo-Saxon Church. *I take great pride in this saint since he bears my name. I know that this is all very childish. If it can be called a fault it is one I share with my son, James. But we have never been able to grow up. St Wilfrid was not much like me at all really. He could be pompous, self-centred and full of his own importance. Well, perhaps that does ring a bell, but not too often I hope.* He was an outstanding evangelist and proclaimed the faith of Christ in a forthright way. He played a significant part in spreading Christianity both in these islands and on the continent. *He did succeed in treading on other peoples' feet from time to time and there is no doubt that it is one characteristic we share.* Wilfrid was consecrated a bishop of all the Northumbrians, perhaps either of Lindisfarne or York or both. His seat was certainly at York. He soon became engaged in the dispute with Theodore at Hertford over the increase in the number of dioceses. He restored and built large churches at York, Ripon and Hexham. As a result of wars, bringing more territory under Northumbrian control, Wilfrid's own ecclesiastical jurisdiction increased.

But in 678AD Wilfrid fell out with King Ecgfrith of Northumbria. The King enlisted the support of Theodore who took advantage of the situation to increase the number of dioceses and created three new bishops for Northumbria. This so affronted Wilfrid that he went to Rome to appeal personally to the Pope. The Pope ruled in Wilfrid's favour so he returned to these shores in 680AD with papal letters designed to ensure his reinstatement to the see of York. But the King would not allow this and instead threw Wilfrid into prison for nine months. He was only released in 681AD provided he left Northumbria.

Wilfrid came south to Sussex and converted many of the heathen there and founded a monastery at Selsey. He also spent time in more western parts and went to the Isle of Wight converting the natives. Wilfrid and Theodore were reconciled in 685AD on the death in battle of King Ecgfrith. The new King of Northumbria, Aldfrith allowed Wilfrid to return as Bishop of York which was now a diocese much reduced in size. Then Wilfrid managed to fall out with Aldfrith and he was again expelled from his see. Aldfrith threatened to destroy Wilfrid by depriving him of all his churches, monasteries and endowments. After Aldfrith's death his successor, Osred, allowed Wilfrid to return and restored all his confiscated property. *Clearly Wilfrid was the proverbial 'difficult man', a bit like myself, some would say.*

Wilfrid did much to establish the Roman Church and its traditions, both by way of widespread conversions to the Christian faith and by helping to eradicate the remaining Celtic traditions. More and more the Church united progressively under the Roman tradition. He introduced a method of chanting in line with the practice of the primitive Church and he introduced also to these islands the monastic rule of St Benedict. By sheer force of character Wilfrid's achievements were great ones. *But he was no politician and was, a bit like myself, a 'bull in a china shop'.* He died in 709AD.

Saint Cuthbert

He was a monk of both the Celtic and Roman traditions. He was born in Northumbria in about 634AD. In 651AD he became a monk at Melrose in the south of Scotland. He then went to Ripon before returning to Melrose. In 664AD he moved to Lindisfarne where he became prior of the religious community. After about eleven years he went to live as a hermit on the tiny island of Farne some seven miles south of Lindisfarne. In 684AD, much against his will, he was made Bishop of Lindisfarne and was consecrated the following year at York. In 687AD after, apparently foreseeing his own death, he retired to Farne Island where he died a little while later.

What has fascinated so many people over the years was the exceptional holiness of Cuthbert, his unsullied quality of life and his powers which, at times, seemed to border on the supernatural. He was a divinely inspired prophet, a healer and his style of life demonstrated a man both of prayer and affinity with the natural world. Whilst he had initially many traits of the Celtic tradition he increasingly adopted Roman practice; he rode on horseback and possessed a magnificent episcopal cross. This was placed on his chest when he was buried and may well demonstrate that the monks around him did not consider such ornateness to be inappropriate. Many miracles were said to have occurred around his grave on Lindisfarne. As the legend grew Cuthbert came to be seen as the 'Wonder-worker of England'.

When the monks came to exhume his body it was said to be incorrupt. This meant that it was hardly decayed, which was regarded as a sign of sanctity. In time a cult grew up to the memory of Cuthbert who was canonised as a saint. Ultimately Cuthbert was reburied in Durham Cathedral which is dedicated to the saint. Some see Cuthbert as the Bishop of Northumbria.

St Cuthbert is also associated with the Lindisfarne Gospels. In a delightful tale, which ought to be true even if it is not, one of the gospels was lost overboard as the monks crossed the Irish Sea. As the monks despaired, a vision of Cuthbert appeared before them and told them where to find the book. It was found on the shore three days later, in the spot foretold by Cuthbert, intact save for some minor staining from the seawater. When the gospel, now in the British Museum, was analysed later, it was found marked with stains that seem likely to be from salt water. So, the romantic tale may contain some truth.

Cuthbert came to be regarded as the greatest symbol of saintliness and spirituality in Anglo-Saxon England. In fact, his status remained unchallenged until the martyrdom of Becket in the 12th century. Thus, he ranks alongside Theodore and Wilfrid as one of the great founders and sustainers of the Christian religion in early times. Whilst his mission was largely of a purely spiritual nature Cuthbert did contribute to the acceptance of the Roman tradition by his adoption of a number of their styles and customs.

The Venerable Bede and other developments

There have naturally been other giants of the early Church. The main one was the Venerable Bede who was both one of the outstanding Christians of the time and was also its major scholar and historian through his Ecclesiastical History of the English People. You will recall that he tells, amongst many other things, the stories of the martyrdom of St Alban and that of the Gregorian mission to England in 597AD restoring in full Roman Christianity. He was born in about 673AD. Bede was responsible for the AD and BC system of dating. He died in 735AD.

Whilst, by the end of the 8th century, the Christian Church was established and flourishing throughout England not everything in the garden was rosy. Shortly before his death Bede was lamenting the state of the Church. He said that it was bedevilled by internal corruption; negligent bishops and clergy, still too many over-large dioceses and, most notably, bogus monasteries. These were a device to avoid military service. The abbots were frequently laymen and the membership of the communities comprised largely renegade monks. They observed no proper religious rule and led a life of wine, women and song. The extent of this corruption was well-known. But it was not until 747AD that a Church Council was held at Clofeshoh (whose precise location is not known today) under the Archbishop of Canterbury, Cuthbert *(not to be confused with the saint: even my son, James, did not make that mistake!)*. The Council addressed all matters needing reform. It demanded that bishops were to visit their dioceses more often to prevent the re-emergence of paganism. They were to examine better the suitability of candidates for ordination and to promote learning; this included enquiring into the private morality of the clergy. In respect of the bogus monasteries the bishops were to conduct visits to ensure that proper monastic rule was being observed. This included the wearing of appropriate dress by the monks and the nuns. In particular the nuns were not to wear 'gaudy, gay clothes such as lay girls use'. The worst of the bogus monasteries were to be dissolved.

England was still divided into a number of Anglo-Saxon kingdoms. At this point the kingdom of Mercia under King Offa (757-796AD) came to dominate the others. Offa had good relations with both the Pope and the Emperor Charlemagne. He was a great benefactor of the Church and founded many monasteries. But Offa's plans for the Church were purely to benefit his own kingdom; he wanted to separate Mercia from the province of Canterbury and give it its own archbishopric. So, at a time when the southern province was starting to act strongly and unitedly in the cause of strong, overall reform, Offa split it into two thus weakening the whole church. Lichfield became an archbishopric with six dioceses at Dunwich, Elmham, Hereford, Leicester, Sherborne, and Worcester falling under its jurisdiction. Canterbury retained London, Rochester, Selsey and Winchester only. This arrangement did not end until 803AD.

THE NINTH CENTURY TO THE NORMAN CONQUEST OF 1066

The Viking invasions

At the end of the 8th century and beginning of the 9th, Norsemen from Scandinavia began to invade England. They were pagans and overran virtually the whole country very quickly. The Christian Church was almost destroyed. The first major monastery to be sacked was Lindisfarne in 793AD. The monks who escaped took with them the bones of St Cuthbert and found a permanent new home at Chester-Le-Street and then Durham. (The remains of St Cuthbert are interred at Durham Cathedral today). One by one the old Anglo-Saxon kingdoms were conquered, including two of the largest, Mercia and Northumbria, until by 870AD only Wessex survived. Monasteries, churches and libraries were all destroyed. Monks and priests were killed or carried into slavery. The saintly Saxon King of East Anglia, Edmund, was killed and became known as St Edmund the Martyr. The outlook for the Christian Church was bleak indeed. It was saved by the efforts of largely one man, Alfred.

Alfred the Great

Alfred was born at the height of the Viking invasions in 848AD. When he ascended the throne of the West Saxons in 871AD at the age of only 22 the whole of England was riven by war and both the Christian religion and learning had been ruined. Alfred's ambition was to restore peace, Christianity and education. He did not have immediate success. He was defeated by a new Viking army. The Vikings advanced progressively further and further into Wessex and Alfred was forced to flee to the westernmost parts of his kingdom. It is here, I think, that legend has it that he met the peasant woman who asked him to mind her baking cakes whilst she went out. Lost in contemplation as to what he had to do to tackle the Vikings he let the cakes burn. On her return the woman boxed him round the ears for his negligence. *I have every sympathy for this lady. Given my own gargantuan appetite for cakes I would have seen this as almost if not an actual hanging offence.*

But despite this unforgivable sin, Alfred hardly put a foot wrong from this point on. He raised fresh troops, marched east and inflicted a heavy defeat on the Danes at Edington and then the surrender of their stronghold at Chippenham. The King of the Vikings, Guthrum, was baptised and agreed to leave Wessex in peace. There then developed a period of uneasy peace with the Danes in command of most of England to the east and north of Watling Street: the Danelaw. Wessex controlled broadly the rest of England. The Vikings mounted a huge invasion towards the end of the 9th Century which it took Alfred and his forces the best part of three years to defeat. Alfred died in 899AD.

But it is not just as a warrior that Alfred is remembered. He played an enormous part in efforts to restore religion and to spread education in the wake of the Viking invasions. His efforts to restore monasteries were thwarted by lack of suitable English monks so that he was obliged to resort to Gaulish ones. They quarrelled so much that Alfred's foundation at Athelney had to close down. But in education he was much more successful.

Alfred was passionate that all his subjects, both noble and those of humbler birth, should be literate. He brought a selection of his subjects together and formed them into a Palace School. Royal officials were compelled to make an effort to educate themselves. Alfred gathered a circle of learned scholars around him. Alfred himself was a highly educated man and he translated from Latin into Old English the Book of Pastoral Rule of Pope Gregory I, the Soliloquies of St Augustine of Hippo and the Consolation of Philosophy by Boerthius. Alfred and his team of scholars also translated Bede's Ecclesiastical History into Old English.

Given all Alfred's immense efforts as a warrior to thwart the Danes and then as a peacemaker, law-giver, statesman and scholar he earned quite rightly the soubriquet 'Great' following his death. Alfred was succeeded by his son, Edward the Elder, who reconquered successfully the Danelaw up to the river Humber. Edward was succeeded by his own son, Athelstan, who was successful in securing the northern border. At the Battle of Brunanburh in 937AD Athelstan defeated armies of both Danes and Scots. Gradually the Danes were absorbed into the overall population of England and converted largely to Christianity. Whilst the remaining years of the 10th century were punctuated by some further Viking invasions effectively England was now a united kingdom, if not, perhaps, a fully stable one.

St Dunstan

Alfred had proved unable to restore the monasteries ravaged by the Viking invasions. The man who did succeed in doing this was St Dunstan born in about 909AD. He became a monk and then in about 943AD the Abbot of Glastonbury. Dunstan was an accomplished scholar, musician and artist. This attracted monks to him from all parts including St Ethelwold, later Bishop of Winchester, and St Oswald, later Bishop of Worcester and Archbishop of York. New monastic houses began then to appear, principally at Abingdon and Westbury-on-Trym, and contacts were established with continental religious houses. The Benedictine rule applied in all these houses. Many monks went on to become bishops and England developed its own peculiar practice known as the 'Cathedral Priory' whereby the diocesan cathedral was manned by monks themselves rather than by secular clergy, the dean and canons. Dunstan's work in restoring the monasteries made him one of the greatest churchmen of his age. It surpassed his achievements as Bishop of Worcester, Bishop of London and finally as Archbishop of Canterbury. As a result of Dunstan's efforts there came into existence about thirty flourishing religious houses for men and about half a dozen for women.

The final part of the Tenth and first part of the Eleventh Centuries

During the 10th century England was, largely, both a united and successful kingdom under the House of Wessex, the descendants of Alfred the Great. Likewise, the Church was established firmly. It was stable and flourishing. The political situation changed at the end of the century when England was ruled by King Ethelred the Unready. Ethelred meant well-advised. 'Unready' was a pun on his name meaning ill-advised. Basically, this meant in '1066 and All That' parlance that he was not a good thing. Danish raids started again towards the end of the century and Ethelred decided stupidly to kill a large number of Danish settlers in what became known as the St Brice's Day massacre. This provoked the Danish king, Sweyn Forkbeard and his son, Cnut, into invading England in 1013AD. Ethelred and his family fled to Normandy for safety. After Sweyn's death in 1014AD Ethelred returned to England but then died. Cnut became King of England in 1016AD. The House of Wessex was deposed but this new invasion did not affect the Church as the Danes were now Christians.

In 1012AD Ælfheah became the first Archbishop of Canterbury to be martyred. He was captured by Viking raiders in 1011AD and killed by them the following year after refusing to allow himself to be ransomed. Ælfheah was canonised as a saint in 1078. Thomas Becket, a later Archbishop of Canterbury, is supposed to have prayed to him just before his own murder in Canterbury Cathedral.

Cnut proved to be an effective ruler of England. Remember he held back the waves!

CANUTE HOLDS BACK THE WAVES NOT ALWAYS SUCCESSFULLY!

My father was a somewhat erratic driver. If he lost concentration he could land himself in a right hole! In the early 1970s he took me and my younger brother, Andrew, out on one of my brass-rubbing expeditions. Brass rubbing was a pursuit of those times, which, since then, has bitten the dust fortunately. It involved going to some church or other, where I could make an image of some medieval knight or ecclesiastic by the rubbing of wax on paper over a brass memorial image. We had just joined a dual-carriageway when I heard suddenly horns blaring and lights flashing. My father realised he was the centre of attention. How could this be so? I think he thought all these cars were driving the wrong way! They obviously thought otherwise. Unlike King Canute my father realised that he was not going to stem the tidal waves of the oncoming traffic. I think when there was a gap in the traffic he simply executed a 'U' turn. How we all survived God alone knows!

Cnut married twice and he had a son by each marriage. His second wife was Emma, the widow of Ethelred by whom she had had two sons, Edward and Alfred. When Ethelred and Emma had returned briefly to England, to challenge Cnut's seizure of the throne, Edward and Alfred remained in exile in Normandy with the royal family there since Emma was a Norman princess. On Cnut's death in 1035AD there followed a power struggle for the throne between his two sons, Harold Harefoot, the son of Cnut's first wife and Harthacnut, his son by Emma, both of whom became king for short periods and died without heirs. In 1042AD the House of Wessex was restored to the English throne in the person of the exiled Edward who became known as Edward the Confessor. It is possible that his restoration was helped by his kinsman, the young Norman Duke, William, who we know as 'The Conqueror'.

Edward the Confessor is a strange man to fathom. He is thought of as the last real Anglo-Saxon king of England, apart from Harold who succeeded him briefly. But Edward was effectively a Norman since he was related to the Norman royal family through his mother. He had been brought up and educated entirely at the Norman court, had received the usual military training and had combat experience. He was by no means the otherworldly character he is seen to be today. He had a fearful temper and could be ruthless in his actions when he wanted to be. Most of his reign was dominated by his dispute with Godwin, the Earl of Wessex, who forced him to marry his daughter, Edith. Edward appointed Normans to English bishoprics including Robert of Jumieges as Archbishop of Canterbury. Godwin overturned this appointment and made a Saxon called Stigand, Archbishop. Edward never had heirs and there is evidence, albeit circumstantial, that he appointed Duke William of Normandy as his successor as early as 1051AD; a factor almost ignored universally when it comes to the Norman invasion of England in 1066. For whatever reason Edward came to be seen as a saint, he was canonised in 1161 and his shrine can be seen in Westminster Abbey to this day. He was the patron saint of England until the 14th century.

On Edward's death at the beginning of 1066 he was succeeded, not by William, but by Harold, Earl Godwin's son. Duke William was, to say the least, not amused. He invaded England to claim what he saw as his own, defeated King Harold at the Battle of Hastings on 14th October 1066 and was then crowned King of England on Christmas Day. *Today 1066, with the possible exception of Magna Carta in 1215, remains the only date in English history that the pig ignorant people of this country recognise in any way. History used to be regarded as important fundamentally and retains that status in other countries. But, like the 'fools' who run the Church of England now, the educational establishment is filled with similar idiots who think the only matters relevant are those relating to 'social issues' alone. God help us all.*

THE NORMAN AND PLANTAGENET CHURCH FROM 1066 TO 1216

The Background

The Norman invasion changed the whole face of England of that there can be no doubt. England ceased to be a country of Scandinavian outlook and became one that looked to northern Europe instead culturally. The Norman invaders were far from being barbarians. They may have been Vikings originally but they had converted long since to Christianity. It was not long before Anglo-Saxon was replaced by Latin as the language of government and the king and nobility spoke Norman-French. The native Anglo-Saxons were seen as second-class citizens but inter-marriage did begin not long after the conquest. Two of the notable chroniclers of the period, Orderic Vitalis and William of Malmesbury, were both of mixed race. Unlike the Saxons the Normans used horses on which to fight and deployed archers extensively. This military practice became naturally that of Norman England. The Normans came to dominate both the administration of the country and the English Church. The Norman nobility came to own most of the land and they built their castles to illustrate their power; castles had hardly existed in Anglo-Saxon England. There was not much that they left untouched and it has affected fundamentally how this country has developed to this day.

In one sense the Church was one of the bodies to be least affected by the Conquest. The Roman Church under the See of Rome continued as before. William had invaded England under the papal banner of Alexander II, as his invasion was considered justified, because he was the rightful heir of Edward the Confessor. He had been accompanied by his formidable half-brother, Bishop Odo of Bayeux, who fought at Hastings with his mighty club. Many saw the invasion as a crusade to establish right. William was a fully conventional churchman. He and his wife, Matilda, had established monastic houses to their memory in the ducal city of Caen; *Aux Hommes* and *Aux Dames.*

So, in the first instance, not much changed. But it certainly did in terms of personnel. In 1170 Archbishop Stigand of Canterbury, a man who had been excommunicated by five successive popes for replacing wrongly his predecessor and, at the same time holding on to his previous post as Bishop of Winchester, the sin of pluralism, was dethroned and imprisoned in chains for life. *I have to say that on many occasions I have felt this to be an appropriate punishment for many bishops of my own time including perhaps the odd archbishop.* The new Archbishop was Lanfranc, the Abbot of Bec, who became one of England's greatest ever archbishops. Generally, William did not trust the existing Saxon holders of high ecclesiastical office and, by the time of his death in 1087, he had replaced most of them with more sound choices. *If only I had ever had that personal power myself.*

The second most obvious change was in the style of ecclesiastical architecture. Anglo-Saxon cathedrals and monasteries were demolished and the stone used to build their great Norman, Romanesque replacements. Some of the finest Norman Cathedrals are at York Minster, Rochester, Durham, Lincoln, Chichester, Winchester, Gloucester and Hereford.

Monasteries continued to flourish during the post-conquest period. Immediately after 1066 there were about 40 religious houses all of which followed the Benedictine rule. Many were rebuilt in the Norman style and monasticism spread rapidly. By 1100 there were well over 100 religious houses, including nunneries, of one type or another. New orders began to arrive in England; the Cluniacs, the White Canons of the Premonstratensian Order, the Augustinians, the Cistercians and the Carthusians. King Henry VIII dissolved the monasteries in the 16th century to obtain their wealth. The ruins of our once great medieval monasteries lie scattered across our countryside today, some of the most famous being Fountains and Rievaulx in Yorkshire and Tintern in Monmouthshire.

All our Norman ecclesiastical buildings are magnificent celebrating the glory of God and his son, Jesus Christ. We do not really know whether they were greater than the Saxon ones they replaced. Some of the latter were also supposed to have been awe-inspiring but none remain other than fragments. *I am sure that the Normans had more than a touch of the Victorian attitude towards building. Most Saxon churches were destroyed; a few survive my own favourite being the wooden church of St Andrew's, Greensted, near Ongar, close to my parish of Chigwell.**

William exercised far greater control of the Church than any of his Anglo-Saxon predecessors. As with the secular part of his realm he would tolerate no opposition. William was also the Duke of Normandy and he brought the English and Norman episcopacy into line with one another. The English bishops became more continentally aware which made them appreciate their valued role as advisers to the king. They and the abbots could not help but be great royal servants, since they owned up to one sixth of England's landed wealth. The bishops were the ecclesiastical part

---

*   The Church at Greensted is not considered now to be as old as first thought.

of England's nobility. Like their lay counterparts they were obliged to provide military service to the king. This necessitated the provision of between as little as two or four but may be as many as fifty or sixty knights for royal service. The larger the number the greater the drain on the bishop's financial resources and the bad effect on the diocese as a whole. We have noted that William's half-brother, Odo, was a fighting bishop and this tradition continued well into the Middle Ages. *I am not too sure that I can imagine many of today's episcopate riding into battle. They are much too weak and feeble and have nothing useful to say.*

The archdeacon was the bishop's chief administrator. The system of archdeacons was extended greatly to improve the management of the Church. Like a latter-day Theodore of Tarsus William rationalised further the diocesan system. Norwich absorbed the dioceses of Elmham and Thetford. Dorchester moved to Lincoln. Lichfield was moved to Chester. Selsey and Sherborne were moved to Chichester and Salisbury where they remain today.

At the other end of the ecclesiastical hierarchy the local clergy were unaffected largely by the Norman invasion. Given their number it was simply not practical to replace them all. They were seen as riff-raff belonging to the agricultural class from which most of them sprang largely. *Nothing much changes. You should see my own family tree and most of us are descended from agricultural labourers.* The English priests in Norman times were uneducated largely and could not conduct services and other aspects of their official duties in anything other than Old English. At this time celibacy was not enforced strictly and the clergy might well be married and have families. This enabled them to leave their benefices to members of their families which was one reason in making the Church adopt a strict prohibition on marriage at a later date. The parochial clergy were a major part of the local community. They never rose to become bishops.

THWARTED AMBITION

My father had undoubtedly no wish to become a bishop. Just as well since there was no chance. My mother used to say that she only married him because she thought he would! My father had the academic talent to be a senior cleric. He preached extremely good sermons (until he got too blasé and insisted on delivering them off the cuff); he was once invited to preach in Westminster Abbey. But he shared the failing which, I think, he handed down to me. Never being able to do and say the right thing, which is just as important, regretfully, in the Church of England as in any other organisation. Father just wanted the church authorities to leave him alone to run his own parish as he saw fit. He came to be seen as a loose cannon who would not co-operate. This was a great shame really since he had more humanity and humility about him than nearly all our current day clergy and bishops put together. I find them almost universally now to be self-satisfied, smug and arrogant. They have no real interest in ordinary Christian people other than as a way to demonstrate their own social awareness and liberalism. If approached they will ensure, no doubt like other professional people are trained to do, against any personal involvement whatever. They are not doctors and solicitors. If they cannot interest themselves in ordinary peoples' lives what real function do they have? These are the people father called the 'fools' and should be destroyed, if not personally, then retired to some 'Guardian' reading care home. Unfortunately, these lunatics are now in charge of the asylum and their position seems unchallengeable.

From 1073 the Pope was Gregory VII. Both he and King William were strong and determined men. Gregory wanted to bring all the rulers of Christendom and their Churches under his strict control. Particularly he wanted all senior ecclesiastical appointments to be subject to his approval. This gave rise to the so-called 'Investiture Contests' where the ruler or the Pope would not accept the other's appointments with the result that the positions might remain vacant for many years. Gregory and William were able to reach a level of understanding. William recognised the value of the relationship with Rome and its importance as part of the wider Christian Church. But William would not accept strict papal control of the church. Certain vacant bishoprics and abbacies were filled up with foreign clergy to fulfil the stricter discipline which Gregory demanded. But the papal demand that William should acknowledge himself as holding England as a fief of Rome met with courteous but unqualified rejection. William, supported by Lanfranc, maintained the right of the King of England to control important ecclesiastical appointments. The row over 'investitures' was to continue well into the 12th century.

Archbishop Lanfranc

We must now talk in more detail about Lanfranc, one of the great Norman Archbishops of Canterbury. He had been abbot of the great monastery of Bec for 20 years and, at the time of his appointment to Canterbury, in 1070 he was the Abbot of St Stephen in Caen, William's own foundation. William and Lanfranc formed a great personal friendship and political alliance. Lanfranc played a vital part in arbitrating favourable terms between William and Pope Gregory in their dispute over the extent of Church authority. Lanfranc was a supremely intelligent man with an intellectual reputation known throughout Europe as well as being a vastly accomplished administrator. He came originally from Pavia in Italy. Lanfranc's main concern was ecclesiastical discipline and the proper enforcement of moral standards amongst the clergy. King William agreed largely with Lanfranc's approach and also saw in him an ally in his rule of England. They did not always see eye to eye, but overall William endorsed his archbishop's strategy.

One major problem was the supremacy of the two Archbishoprics of Canterbury and York. Lanfranc claimed naturally the supremacy of Canterbury, whilst the new Archbishop of York, Thomas of Bayeux, disputed this. Whilst Lanfranc did win the day the issue continued to be one of the great disputes of the Medieval Church in England. Lanfranc extended vastly the system of Church Councils. At these the requirement to appoint archdeacons was enlarged and bishops were to hold synods twice a year. The appointment of more archdeacons was the pre-cursor to the introduction of organised chapters in secularly run cathedrals. The councils also dealt with the rationalisation of the diocesan system. While Lanfranc disapproved of clerical marriage, he realised it was a well-established

English custom and he legislated only to prevent future clerical marriage rather than to make existing married clergy put away their wives.

King William spent most of his reign in Normandy looking after the interests of his duchy. When away he appointed regents, frequently his half-brother, Odo, and sometimes, Lanfranc, to look after England. Latterly Odo disgraced himself by trying to buy the papacy so he could become Pope! When William got wind of this Odo was imprisoned in a dungeon at Rouen. Lanfranc was now in control of England when the king was away. On William's death in 1087 it was to Lanfranc that William Rufus, the King's second surviving son, presented his credentials as the new king on his arrival in England. Lanfranc remained Archbishop of Canterbury until he died in 1089.

King Henry I (1100-1135)

William Rufus died in 1100, whether by way of a stray arrow in a hunting accident or by a plot organised by his younger brother, Henry, we shall never know. Whatever happened Henry became king. He was a ruthless and strong ruler. He is reckoned to have had in excess of 20 children, but they were all largely by women, not his wife, and were illegitimate and could not succeed him. He had only two legitimate heirs, one of whom, the son, William Adelein, was drowned in the 'White Ship' disaster in 1120. His only other legitimate child was a daughter, Matilda. Henry kept the Church, as well as everyone else, under strict control.

His major problem was the succession. His only eligible child was Matilda, who became the Empress due to her marriage to the Holy Roman Emperor, Henry V. After his death Matilda returned to England and she subsequently married Geoffrey of Anjou by whom she had three sons, the eldest of whom was Henry of Anjou. Female rule was virtually unheard of at that time, so Matilda's succession to the English throne, on her father's death, was a tricky one to say the least. King Henry got his nobles to swear allegiance to Matilda on two occasions as his heir.

Archbishop Anselm

Lanfranc's successor was not appointed until 1093. The new Archbishop of Canterbury was Anselm. Like his predecessor he was an Italian and also the current Abbot of Bec. Anselm had come to accept papal authority in a way that Lanfranc had never done. Anselm was no politician. He wished to extend papal authority, including the requirement for papal approval to senior ecclesiastical appointments. There was no way that Henry would agree to this. This revived the 'Investitures Contests' and resulted in a number of bishoprics remaining unfilled for six years or more. Henry's dispute with Anselm went on for seven years. Anselm was exiled twice because of his dispute with royal authority. A compromise was eventually reached by way of the Council of London in 1108 whereby new bishops were to pay homage to the king for the diocesan temporalities, the Church's secular properties and possessions. The bishop's ecclesiastical investiture was within the Church's jurisdiction and was under the authority of the Pope himself. But royal power over appointments remained so that the compromise only affected the method of a new bishop's installation not how he was chosen for office in the first place. Nevertheless, papal power did begin to increase and was only kept at bay by a king of Henry I's calibre. Anselm was a great scholar and theologian who produced two works, the *Monologion* and the *Proslogion,* in which he tried to prove the existence of God by pure reason. In exile he wrote the book *Cur Deus*

Homo? in which he discussed the doctrine of the Incarnation and the Atonement. Anselm died in 1109 and was afterwards canonised as a saint presumably because of his virtuous life and scholasticism.

The Anarchy

But when King Henry died in 1135 Matilda did not become Queen. Before she could cross to England from Anjou she was beaten to it by her first cousin, Stephen, Henry I's nephew. He had the obvious attraction of being a man. The English nobility acclaimed him as king and he was crowned king at Westminster Abbey. Whilst Stephen was undoubtedly a brave warrior he was a weak and useless politician who, to maintain his place on the throne, made increasingly ridiculous promises to restore confiscated land to the church which he was not able to keep. Matilda crossed to England in the late 1130s to fight Stephen for the throne. The civil war swayed this way and that and went on for about 15 years. When Matilda returned to Normandy in about 1149 the war was carried on by her son, Henry of Anjou.

In 1138 Theobald of Bec had been appointed Archbishop of Canterbury. He proved a capable prelate, devout in his private life, charitable and a lover of learning. In political terms Theobald was a wily old fox who tended to support whoever of the two contestants for the throne was on top at particular times. He was apparently loyal to Stephen, but at times he was at Matilda's court. But he worked always for the ultimate succession of Henry of Anjou as king. Theobald made it clear that he would not crown Stephen's son, Eustace of Boulogne, as king. The civil war ended in 1153. Under the Treaty of Winchester of 1153 Stephen was to remain king for life, but, on his death, he was to be succeeded by Henry of Anjou. On Stephen's death the following year Henry of Anjou succeeded quietly to the throne as King Henry II. Henry and his wife, Eleanor of Aquitaine, were crowned King and Queen of England by Theobald in Westminster Abbey in December 1154.

King Henry II (1154-1189)

I regard Henry as possibly the greatest ever of our medieval kings. He was a mighty warrior, a great statesman, administrator and law-giver. In my view he deserves the soubriquet 'Great' in addition to Alfred. *Perhaps it is because he was French by birth that deprived him of the title. This was no different really from all his predecessors since 1066. But we all have our crosses to bear in life. I think the French think much the same of us as we do of them.* Henry's main aim domestically was to restore order to the realm after the civil wars. This embraced both secular and ecclesiastical matters. In his view the Church had obtained far too much independence and power in the chaotic reign of his predecessor. Henry wished to regain control. This was to involve him in one of the greatest disputes of all time; that between himself and his Archbishop of Canterbury, Thomas Becket. Henry's claim to greatness is not based on this event which was largely a disaster, although I think the stance he took was largely sound and his aims were admirable. *He was thwarted by a pig-headed archbishop. Well I think that there have been a few of those. They shall remain nameless of course.*

The Becket Fiasco

When Henry came to the throne in 1154 the Archbishop of Canterbury was still that crafty political operator, Theobald of Bec. He wanted to fight increasing secular control of the

Church at all costs. It was now largely established that the choice of bishops lay with the king. But there were a number of other very important issues that divided the Crown and the Church. The main one was that of 'Criminous Clerks' and 'Benefit of the Clergy'. A custom had developed whereby criminous (accused of a crime) clerks could be tried before secular or ecclesiastical courts, however serious the offence, whether it be unlawful killing, rape, serious assault or arson. If convicted, the clerk could insist on being referred to the ecclesiastical court for sentence. This is what was meant by 'Benefit of the Clergy'. Sentences in the ecclesiastical court were much lower than in the secular court. Whereas murder would be punished probably by a capital sentence in the secular court it could attract only a life sentence in the ecclesiastical court. These largely undesirable church practices had taken hold during the chaotic rule of King Stephen.

King Henry thought that this distinction was without justification. He considered that there was little he could do whilst Theodore remained Archbishop. But Theobald died in 1161 and Henry wanted to take the opportunity to mould the church to his way of thinking. Henry's chancellor and chief minister was Thomas Becket. He was not ordained but had been brought up in Theobald's household where he obtained the best educational opportunities available both in England and on the continent. Theobald himself had recommended him for royal service when Henry came to the throne in 1154. Both Henry and Becket were exceptionally intelligent men who became great friends. It seems that they enjoyed to the full a life together of partying, hunting and the other things that young men do.

Henry decided to appoint Thomas as his new Archbishop of Canterbury. In fairness to Becket it seems he was very reluctant initially, but he did agree eventually. Becket was not yet even a priest, so he was ordained on Saturday 2nd June 1162 before being consecrated Archbishop of Canterbury the following day by Bishop Henry of Winchester. Clearly Becket had only been appointed in order to bring the Church into line with Henry's wishes that 'Benefit of the Clergy' be abolished entirely.

But almost immediately Becket went native, for what precise reasons we shall never know. Maybe he saw his elevation to Canterbury as placing him on a like status to the king from where he could challenge Henry's reforms directly. Whatever his motivation Becket failed totally to cooperate with the king. So, by January 1164, Henry's affection for Becket had cooled considerably. Henry brought matters to a head by the inquest at Clarendon which stipulated that a clerk found guilty before an ecclesiastical court of a crime should be deprived of his holy orders and remitted to the secular court for sentence. Becket remained entirely opposed to this as it went against a cleric's right to be tried and sentenced in an ecclesiastical court according to canon law.

By the Autumn of 1164 there was bitterness and hatred on both sides and Henry contrived deliberately to bring about Becket's ruin by having him tried for secular offences in the royal court. Becket was charged with contempt of the king by failing to obey a summons to answer the complaint of one of the Archbishop's vassals. Becket admitted grudgingly that he had failed to attend. He said he had been sick in bed at the time. *Excuses, it seems, never change.* He was condemned by his brother bishops and sentenced to forfeit his possessions. Becket fled in disguise to the Kent coast and escaped to Flanders where he remained until 1170. He spent most of his exile at Pontigny Abbey in France.

In 1170 Henry decided to follow the European practice and have his eldest son, also Henry, crowned as king. This practice confirmed the right of the son to be his father's successor. The coronation of a king lay in the right of the Archbishop of Canterbury alone but clearly Becket could not execute this since he was in France. Instead on 14th June Henry, the Young King, was crowned in Westminster Abbey by the Archbishop of York, assisted by ten or eleven other English and Norman bishops. This was a clear infringement of Becket's rights, but, surprisingly, Becket did not blame the King for this. He blamed the bishops. Thomas prepared to make peace with the king so that he could pursue the bishops.

Henry and Becket met at Freteval, a castle in Touraine. The terms of an agreement were worked out quickly. Becket was granted leave to take action against the bishops who had crowned the Young King, something that Henry thought would not amount to very much. But when Becket returned to England in October 1170, he excommunicated immediately the bishops who had taken part in the coronation of the Young King. This was a far more severe punishment than Henry had expected. What is more it invalidated the entire coronation ceremony and undermined Henry's plans for the succession. Henry's mood turned to one of cold fury when the bishops told him of Becket's actions.

Henry summoned a Council of the Barons. It is thought now unlikely that he said 'Who will rid me of this turbulent priest?'. Rather he was provoked by one of the barons into responding: 'What idle and miserable men I have encouraged and promoted in my kingdom faithless to their lord, who let me be mocked by this low-born clerk.' Four knights who heard this slipped away and rode to the coast. By the time that Henry realised what they intended to do it was too late to stop them. They murdered Becket in Canterbury Cathedral on 29th December 1170.

We shall, of course, never know what made these men take up Henry's apparent call for Becket to be punished. Whilst Henry was known for his fearsome temper, it was also known that his temper would pass and should not be taken too seriously. Whatever Henry now felt about Becket personally he would have known surely the disastrous political consequences of his Archbishop being murdered apparently on his orders.

The Becket saga disrupted severely Henry's plans to bring order, peace and security to his English realm. Pope Alexander III would not speak to an Englishman for a week! But he did not place an interdict on England or excommunicate Henry personally. Henry was prohibited simply from entering a church until his guilt had been discharged. He, in fact, made himself scarce in Ireland.

Whilst in Ireland Henry received messages from the Papal legates demanding that he meet them. Henry met the legates on 16th May 1172. Henry swore that he had neither desired nor ordered the murder of Becket, but acknowledged that he had caused unintentionally Becket's death by his display of fury at the royal court. He agreed to do penance or other stipulation the legates might make. He was absolved formally of any complicity in the murder of Becket and welcomed back into full membership of the Church. On 12th and 13th July 1174 Henry did penance at Canterbury being scourged by the priests, then passing the night fasting before kneeling at dawn in front of the Archbishop's tomb.

Becket was made a saint on 21st February 1173. Going on pilgrimage to Canterbury to worship at the shrine of St Thomas became part of English medieval life, immortalised to this day by Chaucer's 'The Canterbury Tales'. Pilgrimage to Canterbury continued until the 16th Century when both the shrine and earthly remains of the saint were destroyed under the orders of King Henry VIII. Even though I am not a devoted Becket fan only Henry could have been responsible for such an act of wanton destruction destroying what had become a fundamental part of English medieval culture.

Undoubtedly, Becket had scored a victory for the Church but it was never a substantial one. Certainly, it was true that, by the Peace of Avranches of 1172, Henry had to accept defeat over criminous clerks and the benefit of the clergy and this was to cause problems in the relationship between Church and State right down to the Reformation in the 16th Century. Henry also had to vow not to impede appeals to Rome, but in practice these came to be heard in England by papal judges-legates. Only if it could be proved at the outset that an appeal was malicious could Henry insist that the appellants give security 'that they will seek no wrong to me or disgrace to my kingdom'. The lay courts continued to hold jurisdiction over advowsons, that is, the presentation of priests to benefices in cases of dispute. The Crown's control of appointments to both bishoprics and other senior ecclesiastical appointments was now established, including the actual time when these should be filled when the vacancy arose.

BENEFIT OF THE CLERGY IN MODERN TIMES

You will realise by now that my dear father was a somewhat careless driver. A bit like myself really and I once worked as a taxi-driver! Not for that long! We also shared the habit of breaking the speed limit from time to time. In father's day there were no speed cameras. So, if he was pulled over by the constabulary, instead of getting out of his car, he sat there sulking in his clerical collar. Inevitably, despite his occupation, he was booked, fined and his licence endorsed. Others told him he really ought to chat the police officer up. So, when it happened again, my father immediately got out of the car and charmed the policeman thoroughly. 'I had no idea I was going so fast', he would say. 'I'm so dreadfully sorry'. Usually he drove off uncharged. 'Benefit of the Clergy' had well and truly done the trick. How he would have got on with today's speed cameras I am not sure.

I have always had profoundly mixed feelings about Becket. Why did he feel it so necessary to oppose Henry's eminently sensible proposals for Church reform which he had been appointed to implement specifically? Did he not make this simply an intellectual trial of strength with the king? In one sense I feel that Becket craved his own martyrdom. He achieved what he wanted. But were these issues really worthy of martyrdom?

King John (1199-1216)

Henry II died in 1189 and was succeeded by his son, Richard I, a selfish man, if ever there was one, whose only object was military glory on crusade and latterly defending his father's French empire. Richard was killed, not exercising due care and attention, a bit like my driving, outside the small French fortress of Chalus-Chabrol in 1199. Richard was succeeded by his younger brother, John, who proved to be undoubtedly the most evil man ever to sit on the English throne. Unlike his father and brother he was no soldier. *Cowardice in the face of the enemy were his watchwords.* He tortured his enemies and is thought to have killed personally his 16-year-old nephew, Duke Arthur of Brittany, a close rival for the throne. He was a misogynist who seized women for his own sexual gratification. John was said to have been possibly a non-believer something virtually unheard of for the time. *Non-belief is two a penny today, of course, not least among a goodly number of the ordained ministry I suspect. But, whilst I laugh, it is really no laughing matter.*

The whole of John's family, the Angevins, were highly intelligent and John no less. He lost most of his father's empire in 1204. He spent the next ten years trying to raise the money to mount a successful counter-attack. Whilst no soldier, he was an expert administrator who was adept at turning every cog of the administrative machine to raise extortionate levels of taxation. In relation to the Church John ran into trouble when the existing Archbishop of Canterbury, Hubert Walter, died in 1205. Whilst the right of the king to make ecclesiastical appointments was now established the Pope still tried to intervene in certain circumstances. John instructed the monks at Canterbury to elect as the new Archbishop, John de Gray, Bishop of Norwich. Pope Innocent III vetoed the appointment and insisted that an Englishman called Stephen Langton be elected. Innocent secured Langton's election to Canterbury and crowned him personally as Archbishop at Viterbo north of Rome in 1207.

John was furious and flew into a spectacular Angevin rage. He seized all the lands belonging to Canterbury and expelled the monks who had defied him. In response Innocent imposed an Interdict on England. This was a very heavy sentence since it forbade all church services. The souls of everyone in the land were placed in permanent limbo. Marriages could not be consecrated, baptisms could not take place and the dead could not be buried with the usual Christian rites. Church bells could not be rung. *In certain areas today local residents might see this as a blessing indeed.* The mass went uncelebrated. John was not worried. It was just a great opportunity to confiscate ecclesiastical wealth, lands and property. He was able to extort clerical wealth on a fantastic scale. Innocent tried to increase the pressure on John in 1209 by excommunicating him personally. Every bishop in England then left the realm apart from two of John's closest allies. But John still did not care since the interdict enabled him to increase his normal income by about £100,000 over the course of three years. Whilst John had breached clearly his coronation oath to protect the English Church, he was now a very rich king.

On 13th May 1213 John met the papal legate, Pandulf Verraccio, and agreed to return to the Church. He accepted Stephen Langton as Archbishop of Canterbury. Extraordinarily he also agreed to hand over England and Ireland as fiefs to the papacy and to pay the Pope an annual tribute of 1,000 marks, about £666. John submitted humbly then to papal control. This meant that he could no longer extort the church financially and must have caused him some personal loss of pride. So, what were the reasons for John's extraordinary about-turn? John could now claim special protection from all his enemies as a personal vassal of the Pope. In 1214 John launched his European counter-attack. On 27th July John's allies met the French King Philip Augustus at the tiny village of Bouvines in Flanders and were routed completely. John had to return to an England now bankrupt and on the verge of civil war. In a remarkable act of cynicism John took the solemn oath of a crusader in March 1215. John had no intention of going to the Holy Land; what he did was simply a device to gain further papal favour and to deter enemies from attacking him. Civil War, led by the barons, did erupt and culminated in the great confrontation with the king at Runnymede Green leading to the signing of Magna Carta. The Archbishop of Canterbury, Stephen Langton, was to play a crucial role as a mediator and negotiator between the king and the barons at Runnymede. Whilst Magna Carta is remembered chiefly now for its provisions requiring that all freemen should be tried by their peers before deprivation of their liberty or lands, its first clause declares that the English Church shall be free. This meant that it should be free to elect all its officers according to canon law. John quickly rebutted the charter, with the support of the Pope, who excommunicated now all the rebel barons, which led to the renewal of civil war. By the time of John's death in 1216 England had been invaded and occupied substantially by the French.

There is some doubt as to whether England's enfeoffment to the Papacy and liability for the indemnity, which went with it, were ever revoked. In which case there may be billions of pounds, when compound interest is taken into account, owing to the Holy Father today. Perhaps this should be top of the agenda at the next meeting between the Archbishop of Canterbury and the Pope!

THE ENGLISH CHURCH FROM 1216 TO THE BREAK WITH ROME IN 1532-1534

The Thirteenth Century

In 1216 John was succeeded by his 9-year-old son, known as King Henry III (1216-1272). He was too young to rule initially and the regent was the 70-year-old, but still physically mighty, William Marshal, Earl of Pembroke. He was instrumental in re-establishing royal rule which had broken down during John's tyrannical reign, resulting in all-out civil war and the French invasion to support the rebel barons. The Marshal had the young king crowned immediately, at was then Gloucester Abbey, and in 1217 led an army personally into battle at Lincoln where he defeated the French roundly. As a result of their defeat the French came to terms rapidly and left the country.

John's enfeoffment of England to the papacy meant that the country was infested with papal legates, *a truly delightful concept I think,* during Henry's reign trying to enforce papal sovereignty. Whilst these men helped to stabilise England their presence became increasingly resented, particularly, when Henry himself turned to these legates for advice exclusively. Many came to see this situation as England being subject to direct rule from Rome. The Pope, Innocent III, was determined to establish papal supremacy over all the powers in western Christendom falling under his jurisdiction. In order to establish this authority he needed ever-increasing amounts of money. Not only did the

Pope rely on taxation he introduced a system known as 'provisions'.

There was now an ever-increasing number of ecclesiastical appointees, all of whom needed to be paid. So, what better way of solving the problem than by appointing them to church positions from which they could draw substantial remuneration. There would be no work of course. Where limited to appointments to canonries and to prebendaries, either at cathedrals or collegiate churches, the system's scope for abuse was quite limited. But, in respect of normal church livings, substantial corruption arose. Frequently those 'provided' to country benefices were total absentees. They included young, barely adolescent Italian boys and Italian papal chaplains, none of whom would ever set foot outside Italy. An enormous amount of money was lost to the church in supporting this foreign, religious establishment. But the iniquitous system of 'provisions' was not abolished until the middle of the 14th century when the Statute of Provisors of 1351 was enacted.

Unfortunately, God's Church has been subject to many other abuses. Some abuses related to pluralism (holding more than one appointment at the same time) and absenteeism (never turning up at all). Efforts were made to improve clerical education and dress. Additionally, the clergy were encouraged to give more attention to their duties. *Less time was to be spent down the pub and, perish the thought, with the local young ladies.* The Church rebuked both its clergy and the laity for their sometimes lax and immoral standards of behaviour. The laity were reprimanded for their non-attendance at church. *No doubt the threat of hell-fire and damnation made most of them take notice. I am afraid that there is no chance of that today. The laity will now just have to burn in Hell when they get there.* Statutes were issued to ensure that church services were ordered properly, that there were sufficient orders of service and that there were sufficient and suitable church ornaments.

ESSENTIAL PASTORAL CARE

My father, throughout his life, enjoyed his visits to hostelries, either locally or on holiday for a couple of drinks and a good meal. Unlike myself he never drank much. But, on one occasion he did say, at the top of his voice, in the pub itself that he was 'paralytic'. He did not know the meaning of the word. All he meant was that he had had one more than his usual and was feeling a bit 'tiddly'. At his last parish of Hatfield Heath he did start holding a brief Harvest Festival service at the 'White Horse' Inn. Whether the regulars truly enjoyed this was another matter altogether!

Whilst Henry III was a rather weak king, he was a devout son of the Church and made a major contribution to Church architecture. He was obsessed with the cult of St Edward the Confessor who had been made England's patron saint since 1161. Few, if anybody now, seems to know why Edward was canonised. Henry decided that the existing Westminster Abbey was not a suitable building to house the shrine to the saint. Henry constructed both a new shrine to Edward the Confessor and a new abbey building in which it should be housed. That building, in the Gothic and Perpendicular style, is the Westminster Abbey we see today. *But who built the previous round-arch, Romanesque building, that the new abbey replaced? Well, it was no less than Edward the Confessor himself. Somewhat ironic, I think. Perhaps Henry was a true 'Victorian'.*

Henry's son Edward I (1272-1307) was a truly formidable man and warrior. He conquered all of Wales and had completed nearly the conquest of Scotland by the time of his death. He tightened substantially the Crown's control of the Church, so that it did not become unduly influential as it had done in the time of his father. His most controversial religious action was to expel the Jews in 1290, so he could seize their land and money. The expulsion was carried out with considerable brutality and the Jews were not allowed back to England until the time of Oliver Cromwell in 1655.

The 14th Century

The power of the papacy became more and more unpopular as the 14th century unfolded due to its ever-increasing demands for money to finance its political and military schemes. Legislation was enacted in England to curb papal power. I have mentioned the Statute of Provisors of 1351 which abolished the corrupt system of 'provisions'. Two years later there followed the First Statute of Praemunire of 1353 prohibiting appeals to the Pope where a proper English court had already jurisdiction to deal with the matter. Those in breach of this law were punishable by outlawry.

The heavy punishment of outlawry was extended in 1365 to those seeking from Rome benefices or citations. The ancient practice of paying 'Peter's Pence' was for a time suspended; this was an annual tax of a penny paid by landowners to the papal treasury in Rome. It had been instituted during the 7th or 8th century and continued until the 16th century. The laws against provisors and praemunire were also tightened in 1390 and 1393.

Not only aspects of papal rule were corrupt. There were plenty of examples much closer to home involving the abusive behaviour of bishops, parochial clergy, monks and friars towards the poor, downtrodden and the oppressed. In

Piers Plowman William Langland attacks the friars and the clergy for the abuses of the church:-

> *I found there friars · of all the four orders,*
> *Preaching to the people · for profit to themselves,*
> *Explaining the Gospel · just as they liked,*
> *To get clothes for themselves · they construed it as they would.*
> *Many of these master friars · may dress as they will,*
> *For money and their preaching · both go together.*
> *For since charity hath been chapman · and chief to shrive lords,*
> *Many miracles have happened · within a few years.*
> *Except Holy Church and they · agree better together,*
> *Great mischief on earth · is mounting up fast.*
>
> *There preached a pardoner · as if he priest were:*
> *He brought forth a brief · with bishops' seals thereon,*
> *And said that himself · might absolve them all*
> *From falseness in fasting and of broken vows.*
>
> *Parsons and parish priests · complained to the bishop*
> *That their parishes were poor · since the pestilence time,*
> *And asked leave and licence · in London to dwell*
> *And sing requiems for stipends · for silver is sweet.*

The author personifies the parson as 'Sloth' who, despite thirty years in his parish, could not read a line of his books. *Naturally, he was highly skilled in field sports.*

In the mid-14th century England was afflicted by the terrible Black Death. The bubonic plague appeared first in 1348 and lasted through to about 1352. England had then a population of about five million people. Whilst nobody knows precisely how many died, some say that up to half the population was wiped out. Naturally the clergy were affected particularly badly since they were ministering closely to the sick and dying all the time.

Ecclesiastical Organisation in the 13th and 14th Centuries

I will now look at how the church was organised both at its highest and lowest levels. During this period there were seventeen dioceses in England and four in Wales. They varied greatly in size. There were two vast dioceses; firstly, Lincoln, which stretched over eight counties from the Humber to the Thames and, secondly, York, which stretched from the west coast of Cumbria to Nottingham. The two smallest were Rochester and Worcester. Each diocese was then divided into two or more archdeaconries which were then sub-divided into a number of rural deaneries. These basic administrative units remain to this day.

The vast diocesan cathedrals were not intended for large gatherings of diocesan clergy and laity; they were meant as grand and dignified settings in which priests might offer daily worship, of the highest ceremony and devotion, to God. If you visit any major cathedral city today you will find, in addition to the cathedral church, many other parish churches for use by the ordinary people. Today a good many of these are likely to be redundant for ecclesiastical purposes and the buildings will be used as art galleries or museums. There were fifteen diocesan cathedrals; eight were monastic foundations and seven secular. Not surprisingly the bishop of a monastic foundation was invariably a monk. Towards the end of the 13th century a number of friars were appointed, most notably two Archbishops of Canterbury, Robert Kilwardby and John Pecham.

Many bishops were distinguished academics and able administrators. But the majority of bishops were royal favourites, who wished to be at court, currying favour with the king, rather than in their dioceses. They left most of their church work to others. The bishop became a major landowner once appointed. His estate comprised frequently many manors whose resources were necessary to feed the bishop's substantial household. Bishops, who served their dioceses faithfully, led an itinerant life conducting diocesan business as they went. They visited parishes, interviewed the clergy, examined the books and ornaments of the churches and listened to evidence from the laity as to parochial matters. Those monastic chapters, still subject to episcopal control, were also subject to visitation by the bishop. It was possible for confirmations to be held on episcopal visits, but most medieval bishops were reluctant to confirm children. Ordinations might also take place.

The bishop spent the greater part of his time presiding over a court, hearing cases against both clergy and laity who had broken church law. Those clerics, who were found not to have carried out their duties properly, were liable to a fine, suspension, deprivation of their benefices and sometimes imprisonment. Lay people, found guilty of infringing the moral laws of the church, could be sentenced to public flogging by the rural dean. *I am rather amused by the idea of rural deans today, particularly one or two gentle souls I have known, lashing offenders half to death.*

The parish priest was always known initially as the 'rector' from the Latin meaning ruler. He was the incumbent of his living which he enjoyed as a freehold. There developed then a system called 'appropriations' in which the patron of the living, some kind of bigwig either locally or elsewhere, gave it away usually to a monastery, so great was the desire at this time to found or support religious houses. The financial benefit to the monks was substantial as they could arrange for a stipendiary priest, who in time came to be known as a vicar, an assistant to a superior, from the Latin, *vicarious*, to do the work of the parish for a very low sum whilst keeping the remaining income of the living for themselves. Whilst, a system of 'vicarages' was introduced in the 13th century, which tried to ensure that the vicar had a definite stipend and security of tenure, his wage remained very low and the monasteries continued to gain very substantially. The terms 'rector' and 'vicar' remain today, but there is now no real difference between the two.

Where churches remained non-appropriated the parishes continued to be served by rectors. The majority of these were local men drawn from the upper ranks of the peasantry and the artisans and were not educated particularly well. They lived off the land, much as their parishioners did. But a minority of the rector class were wealthy men who held at least more than one living. They came frequently from rich families and they regarded their benefices simply as a source of income. Like the monasteries they employed vicars to do the actual parochial work. Some rectors became immensely rich as there was no limit to the number of livings they might hold. Many were not ordained as there was never any need to visit their parishes. Others might be boys at school or university and they paid their tuition fees out of the profits of their livings.

The value of livings varied enormously in the middle ages. Some might be worth as little as three or four pounds a year, but a few could be worth several hundreds. The average gross income came partly from the land and partly from the offerings of the people. Every parish church was supposed to have attached to it some land called 'glebe' which the rector held as freehold and which he farmed himself with assistance from his page. *Glebe land still exists to this day and I had a substantial glebe field at my parish of Chigwell on part of which the new vicarage was built.*

The most important part of a parish priest's income was from tithing. This was his right to a tenth of all natural produce within his parish whether from crops or plants grown in the soil or from livestock, mainly, cows, sheep, pigs, goats and others.

PAY DAY

My father certainly did not become a clergyman for the money. The stipend, as it was called in his day, was pitifully low. The only much-needed supplement to this income was from his fees for weddings and funerals plus his small income as a part-time Religious Instruction teacher at Chigwell School. My mother also used to teach part-time. My father's great bonus every year was on Easter Day when the church collection, known as the Easter Offering, went directly to the priest. My father's parish was a wealthy one, so he got a substantial sum every year. You can imagine his disappointment when the Church of England decided to discontinue this system, no doubt in the name of some false notion of fairness. I believe some form of central distribution was substituted. Well, I suppose the new system was fairer. But we Tories are not that good on equality, frequently because it does not work! The decision to cancel my father's well-earned benefit was no doubt decided on by some 'fools' somewhere or other!

The most important tithes were those against corn, hay, vegetables and fallen timber. Animal tithes were enforced by way of levy on animal produce; milk, eggs, butter, cheese, honey and wax. Where there were practical difficulties in enforcing the tithes they were commuted to a payment in lieu. It was artisans and other traders who bore the brunt of the tithing system since payment was taken from their profits and wages. Tithing was a lucrative and much hated system. Tithing continued well into modern times and was always resented highly. It did not finally come to an end until well into the 20th century and, even now, it still arises occasionally say with liability to Chancel Tax which emerges sometimes in domestic conveyancing transactions. *Whilst I can understand that this was not a popular system, due to the way it operated, I cannot help thinking that people spend their money willingly on anything provided it has nothing to do with Mother Church.*

Not all church income belonged to the parish priest. It was supposed to be divided between the priest and the bishop. It was also to be used for church maintenance and poor relief. Keeping a medieval church upright remains one of the major pre-occupations of parish life today; the crumbling tower, the disintegrating fabric, the leaking roof and the replacement of the ancient organ which, of course, the organist deems essential. All this gives rise to a constant round of fund-raising appeals and other money raising activities. It is a fact of life that our great medieval churches require constant maintenance. Some think that the money would be spent better on the poor. But remember these ancient places are great monuments to Christian worship throughout the ages. They must not be allowed to crumble. They are of inherent and irreplaceable value. Failure to maintain these buildings will not resolve the problem of poverty.

Whilst William Langland attacked the friars and clergy for abusing their calling in 'Piers Plowman' it is clear that not all priests were feckless individuals. Geoffrey Chaucer shows a parson of genuine belief and devotion to his duties in 'The Parson's Tale':-

He was a shepherde and noght a mercenarie.
And thogh he hooly were and vertuous,
He was to synful men nat despitous,
Ne of his speche daungerous ne digne,
But in his techyng discreet and benynge.

Chaucer's parson is also no respecter of persons in demanding ultimate adherence to moral principles:-

But it were any person obstinat,
What so he were, of heigh or lough estat,
Hym wolde he snybben sharply for the nonys.
(But if some sinful one proved obstinate,
Whoever, of high or low financial state,
He put to sharp rebuke, to say the least.)

None of the explicit criticism of the clergy that marks many of the other tales and character sketches is obvious here. The parson is throughout depicted as a sensible and intelligent person. *Much like myself of course.*

The Friars

The friars were a new type of religious order who appeared at the beginning of the 13th century. Whilst under religious discipline, they were free to go amongst people wherever they were to minister the Christian faith. The two greatest orders were the Dominicans and the Franciscans. It was the Franciscans who were inspired by St Francis of Assisi. He dedicated his life to espousing the life led by Christ as did his disciples; poverty, humility and suffering. They arrived in England in 1221 and Archbishop Stephen Langton was very impressed by their demeanour and preaching skills.

The friars soon spread throughout England preaching the gospel of Christ and establishing their own religious houses. This filled a void in most parish churches where the ordinary clergy simply did not have the ability to preach. The standard of parochial worship was immeasurably improved. Many friars settled initially into the academic world of Oxford and Cambridge, so young friars could obtain the best education available and young students would be attracted into joining their orders.

But, as time progressed, the friars lost sight increasingly of their vocation. They wanted larger and larger religious houses incorporating vast libraries for themselves. As their only means of income was begging, the practice became corrupt so as to maximise the financial return. The friars began to keep servants, eat more exotic food and live in more and more luxurious conditions. They came to be seen as a menace in the way they seized wrongly from ordinary parish priests the right to preach sermons, hear confessions and conduct funeral rites all in return for payment. The Pope intervened in 1300 providing that friars had to be licensed before preaching or hearing confessions and they were obliged to pay a proportion of all funeral offerings to the parish priest. We have seen what William Lackland had to say about the friars in Piers Plowman. But they had been initially a force for good and had contributed in a most positive way to the well-being of the church.

The conventional Monastic Houses

Monasteries did begin to decline during this period since few new religious houses were built. Monastic life was bound by ascetic rules in the vows of celibacy, poverty, and obedience. The daily life of a monk was encapsulated into a cycle of prayer and praise. It also incorporated a programme of sacred study and many monasteries developed large libraries. Despite the vow of poverty, monasteries became increasingly wealthy because rich barons gave them land and endowments and they were centres of the wool trade. But the monasteries began to lose their initiative in scholarship to the universities and the friars and ceased to be the great centres of learning they once had been. Monastic decline was accelerated also by the Black Death and, by the end of the 14th Century, most of the great monastic houses were half empty.

As the monks became more wealthy and owned more land they found themselves obliged to serve the Crown. They had to spend more and more of their time devoted to earthly business matters rather than to God. The monastic way of life began to change fundamentally and earthly pleasure in one form or another replaced the previously austere way of life. In the end most of the senior abbots had seats in the House of Lords and lived the life of Riley; hunting and hawking and wining and dining lavishly in their own houses away from their monks. *I have to admit this sounds very appealing to me. Seriously, by the time of the break with Rome in the 16th century, monastic standards of behaviour had dropped very considerably and were used as an excuse by King Henry VIII to order the dissolution of the monasteries.*

Lollardy

An important religious movement developed in the 14th century known as Lollardy. It was not an organised movement. Lollards were simply people brought together by an informal set of beliefs. Those beliefs varied in focus and intensity from one person to another.

The origins of Lollardy can be traced to the writings of John Wycliffe. Wycliffe was a churchman, writer, and theologian who was born sometime in the 1320s and died on the last day of 1384. Wycliffe believed that the church had drifted away from its purely spiritual foundations and, further, that it should have no part to play in worldly affairs. He was strongly critical of papal influence in secular life and sought to make religious teachings more accessible to everyone. He thought that the Bible and the Church's scriptures should be translated into English so that they could be read and understood by everyone. Wycliffe began a translation of the Bible into English. But later on such translations were made illegal.

Lollardy believed that the only true source of doctrine and the only relevant measure of legitimacy was the Bible itself. Lollardy rejected the Roman Catholic doctrine of the real presence of Christ in the eucharist known as transubstantiation. The Lollards rejected also the doctrine of purgatory. They believed that priestly celibacy was an invention of the Antichrist. They did not believe the practices of baptism and confession were necessary for salvation. Oaths, fasting, and prayers for the dead were thought to have no scriptural basis. They had a poor opinion of the trappings of the Catholic church; holy bread, holy water, bells, organs, church buildings for example. They rejected the value of papal pardons. The sixteenth century martyrologist, John Foxe, described the main beliefs of Lollardy: opposition to pilgrimages and saint worship, denial of the doctrine of transubstantiation and a demand for English translation of the scriptures.

The Lollards believed that the Catholic Church had been corrupted by temporal matters and that its claim to be the true church was not justified. Part of this corruption involved prayers for the dead and chantries. These were seen as corrupt since they distracted priests from other work and that everyone was entitled to be prayed for equally. Believing in a universal priesthood the Lollards challenged the Church's authority to invest or deny the divine authority to make a man a priest. Denying any special status to the priesthood, Lollards thought confession to a priest was unnecessary, since they believed that priests did not have the ability to forgive sins. Lollards believed priests should not hold government positions as such worldly matters would interfere likely with their spiritual mission.

Both the Crown and the nobility came to see Lollardy as a threat to their existence, an incitement to upheaval and rebellion. But, following Wycliffe's death in 1384, Lollardy lasted until well into the following century. Some say that its ideas may have contributed to the English reformation in the 16th century. Whilst this may well overstate the case greatly its ideas, in relation to prayers for the dead and the status of the priesthood, may have had some influence.

The early years of the Sixteenth Century until the Break with Rome in the early 1530s

The 15th century was not a significant one for church history itself. In secular history events were dominated by the second part of the 100 Years' War against the French. *Like the first part in the 14th century England won the battles; Agincourt, like Crecy and Poitiers before it, but lost the wars after which the English were ejected from France unceremoniously.* This period was followed by the domestic civil wars known as 'The Wars of the Roses'. These culminated in 1485 when Henry Tudor came to the throne as King Henry VII of England after the Battle of Bosworth.

In 1509 Henry Tudor died and was succeeded by his son, King Henry VIII, the one king in English history of whom most people know something; his six wives, his obesity and his psychopathic ruthlessness towards his enemies. But when he came to the throne he was a Renaissance prince; tall and handsome, athletic, highly educated and a devout and true son of the Roman Catholic Church.

As king, Henry wrote a book called *Assertio Septem Sacramentorum,* (Defence of the Seven Sacraments). This book defended the sacramental nature of marriage and papal supremacy. It is also known as the 'Henrician Affirmation' and was written to reject the ideas of the Protestant Reformation, especially those of Martin Luther. This was seen as a supreme act of loyalty to the Roman Church for which in 1521 Henry was awarded the title, 'Defender of the Faith', by Pope Leo X. The title remains a subsidiary one of English and then British monarchs to this day. When Henry broke with Rome in the early 1530s, it was a political rather than religious act and the king remained effectively a good catholic for the rest of his days.

For the first twenty years of Henry's reign, which was after all the majority, England remained part of the Roman Catholic Church. Henry had the assistance of a powerful and high-ranking ecclesiastic to help him with the day to day running of the realm. He was Thomas Wolsey, the Cardinal Archbishop of York. Wolsey was more a politician than a churchman. His power, at its height, was almost absolute, second only to the king himself. He enabled his master to pursue his personal pleasures as much as possible. He only fell from power when he could not obtain an annulment to Henry's first marriage to Catherine of Aragon, so that he could re-marry to beget male heirs. Henry VIII broke then with the Roman Church to secure the dissolution of his marriage. The sun had set for good on the Roman Catholic Church's authority over England, other than the brief revival under Mary Tudor in the 1550s.

JUNE

THE LEGACY OF THE ROMAN CATHOLIC CHURCH

General

The legacy the Anglican Church owes to the Roman Catholic Church is substantial. As early as Roman times we have seen the beginnings of the forms of belief and clerical organisation that still exist today. Both the Apostles' and Nicene Creed originated at this time. Additionally, the basic ecclesiastical orders of bishops, priests and deacons came into being.

Architecture

In both Saxon and Norman times magnificent buildings, both churches and cathedrals, were built. No Saxon cathedrals remain and very few churches since they were destroyed largely by the Normans after the invasion of 1066. The finest remaining Saxon church in the country is All Saints' Church, Brixworth, Northamptonshire which is still wholly intact and was built about 670AD using bricks from a nearby Roman villa. I will mention also St Martin's Church at Canterbury in Kent. Not only is this an example of a surviving Saxon church, in addition it has remains of an earlier Christian place of worship from Roman times thus making it one of the oldest known churches in the country.

Whilst the Normans may have destroyed largely the Saxon architectural legacy, they left a magnificent collection of Romanesque round-arch cathedrals, monasteries and churches of their own. I have mentioned already a number of these great buildings. The Norman style of architecture developed after the 12th century into the Gothic, Perpendicular and Early English styles, some of the most famous of which can be found at Westminster Abbey, Ely and Salisbury cathedrals. Subsequently there came about the peculiarly English style of medieval ceiling construction known as fan vaulting, two of the most outstanding examples of which are at King's College Chapel, Cambridge and the King Henry VII Chapel at Westminster Abbey. All in all, I hope you can see that we owe a great debt to the Roman Church for the awe-inspiring buildings built under her auspices.

Church Organisation

The Roman Church defined Church organisation as we know it today. The two archbishoprics at Canterbury and York were brought into being many centuries before the reformation of the 16th century. Initially York fought Canterbury as to precedence, but it has been long now accepted that the Archbishop of Canterbury is the senior churchman of the English Church, the Primate of all England. The Archbishop of York is the second senior churchman and is the Primate of England.

At the time of the break with Rome there were about seventeen dioceses in England. Today there are over forty. The medieval bishops were expected to visit and inspect the parishes and monasteries under their jurisdiction. In order to assist them the post of archdeacon was introduced which remains to this day. Below the archdeacon there came about groupings of parishes under a rural dean. Again, this remains part of church organisation now. *Remember the rural dean was to flog ecclesiastical lay offenders. So, watch out, watch out if there is a rural dean about!*

We owe the fundamental part of our ordinary parochial structure to the period of the Roman Church. As long ago as the time of the Venerable Bede he wrote that there ought to be a parish priest in every town, a system which persists in our local parishes. Some parishes came about from the small, private chapels, known as oratories, owned by a local lord. The bishops tried to ensure that this system was not abused by this practice and ensured that provision was made for a proper local priest. The bishop held both the lands over which the local church had been built and dedicated and also the tithes and other general ecclesiastical contributions known, in medieval times, as 'Church-shot'. Local administration of the tithes and other matters was delegated by the bishop to the parish priest who obtained the freehold of his living. This is the origin of the system today, where local parish priests are said to occupy their livings as freeholders. Until the 1970s, when the church introduced a compulsory retirement age for all new priests, a parish priest could hold his parish for life. We have seen why parish priests were called 'rectors' and 'vicars' a distinction that means almost nothing today.

Liturgy

When Augustine re-introduced Roman Catholicism to England in 597AD there was no universal Roman liturgy. There were a number of rites in use throughout the western Roman Church and they continued to be used broadly until about the 11th century. Further forms of the Roman rite developed then throughout the rest of the middle ages. Undoubtedly Augustine used nothing other than the mass he had used in Rome. The mass would have been in Latin and not the vernacular. The term 'mass' is the English version of the Latin term *'missa'*. In Latin the Mass ends with *'Ite missa est'*, which in English translates as 'Go, it is sent'; 'it' means the Church. From the Latin *'missa'* comes the English word 'dismiss'. So, the 'Mass' means 'dismissal', which is equivalent to where 'The Blessing' in our Anglican church services takes place today.

From earliest times the Mass commenced with the celebrant and other ministers processing to the altar where a psalm in Latin was sung. They came down then from the altar for the reading of the gospel. It is possible a litany was sung between the introit and the collect. It is not known whether the gloria was sung in earliest times. The gospel procession was one of great ceremony; the clergy bore lights and incense and walked down the nave to the pulpit where the standing people bowed deeply to the gospel book. After the gospel a sermon might be preached. The creed was said rather than sung as in later times. A collection might be taken from the people. The consecration of the bread and wine took place then which was distributed to the congregation. The service finished with the dismissal.

I hope that this shows that the framework of the Anglican Holy Communion service today derives both from the earliest usages of the Roman Church and the changes in Catholic liturgy that developed later on. This is despite the major doctrinal differences between the Roman Catholic and Protestant communions which now exist. We may not use such lavish ceremony as the Roman Church, but our Anglo-Catholic friends more than make up for that. Since the time that Thomas Cranmer introduced the first Anglican prayer book in 1549 our services today are in English. The basic format remains the same today despite the best efforts of our liturgical reformers.

All Anglican prayer books contain forms of service for Morning Prayer (Matins) and Evening Prayer (Evensong). These derive from the ancient monastic offices of Matins/Lauds and Vespers/Compline respectively. Where these offices were sung it brought about a distinctive Anglican chant applied to canticles and psalms. Plainsong was used often as well. By late medieval times many English cathedrals and monasteries had established small choirs of trained lay clerks and boy choristers to perform polyphonic settings of the Mass in their lady chapels. This choral tradition has persisted down the ages to recent times. Fully robed and surpliced choirs began to lead the services from specially constructed stalls in the chancel.

Doctrine

Most importantly, Anglicanism draws strongly from its Roman Catholic Church heritage in relation to doctrinal matters. This is seen in the importance that the Church of England places on the sacraments as a means of grace, sanctification and salvation, as expressed in the Church's liturgy and doctrine. All Anglicans recognise baptism and the eucharist as being instituted directly by Christ. Of the other five; confession and absolution, matrimony, confirmation, ordination and unction (anointing of the sick) the Anglo-Catholics, particularly, see them as full sacraments. But, many broad- church and low-church Anglicans regard them simply as 'sacramental rites'.

THE REFORMATION IN THE 16TH CENTURY

Martin Luther nailed his Ninety-five Theses to the door of All Saints' Cathedral in Wittenberg on 31 October 1517. This was effectively the start of the Protestant Reformation. Luther's protest was against specifically the Catholic Church's sale of indulgences, a means by which sins were forgiven. Indulgences were granted initially either in return for the saying of a prayer or the performance of good works. The system became corrupt increasingly by the sale of indulgences for larger and larger sums of money to swell church coffers. Matters came to a head when the Pope used this device to fund the re-building works at St Peter's Basilica in Rome.

There were many other causes of discontent with the Roman Church. One was the sale of holy relics. *I have a very big nose, no doubt like St Wilfrid's himself, which would have made a fine relic. I am sure it would have raised thousands of pounds. But its actual holiness, not just the nose, but the person it belonged to, is somewhat doubtful I think.* Additionally, the greed and scandalous lives of the clergy created a split between them and their parishioners. Frequently they did not speak the local dialect or language or live in their actual parish. There was still too much pluralism and simony, that is, the sale of church offices. Doctrinally Martin Luther came to believe in the primacy of faith over good works, and in the priesthood of individual believers. Luther's challenge produced a storm within the Church that eventually drove him to reject some other Catholic doctrine and organise his own church.

He did not, in fact, reject transubstantiation. Luther was excommunicated in 1521, but became a national hero under the protection of the Elector of Saxony, and soon other German princes joined the Protestant movement.

The Break with Rome

In England the matter developed in an altogether different way. King Henry VIII was a young, glamorous renaissance prince when he became king in 1509. *He was tall, learned and athletic, not qualities that I ever had very much to worry about. Although I do like to think I have a little learning.* Henry was also an absolutely loyal son of the Roman Catholic Church. He was as different as could be from the obese man that he became by the end of his reign in 1547.

Whilst the same forms of Church corruption were present in England, as in Europe generally, and there was protest, as echoed by the Lollardy movement of the 14th and early 15th centuries, none of this was relevant so far as King Henry was concerned. Henry VIII's wish to break with Rome was due to what he saw as his need to divorce his first wife, Catherine of Aragon, and marry Anne Boleyn. But, whilst this is broadly true, there was a great deal more to it than sex and lust, qualities with which the king is identified mostly today. What Henry was interested in really was obtaining male heirs to succeed him to secure the Tudor dynasty. His father, Henry VII, had overthrown the last Plantagenet king, Richard III, at the Battle of Bosworth in 1485. But many still challenged the right of the Tudor family to hold the throne. Henry wanted desperately a son to carry on the Tudor line after his death. When he became king in 1509 he married his elder brother's widow, Catherine of Aragon. Since Catherine had been married to his elder brother, Papal Dispensation was necessary, as canon law prohibited a man from marrying his brother's widow. This was granted. The union, at first, was very happy. But no sons were born, only a daughter, Mary. As the 1520s began Catherine was nearing 40 and it was becoming very unlikely that any further child would appear.

Henry decided now that he must have a new wife. Whilst divorce as such was well-nigh impossible, annulments of royal marriages were granted on a regular basis. The usual ground relied on was that the parties were too closely related. Virtually any degree of relationship raised that possibility. But it was not so in this case and the king decided to revisit the issue of the marriage to his brother's widow. Leviticus (Ch18v16) says that 'Thou shalt not uncover the nakedness of thy brother's wife: it is thy brother's nakedness'. It goes on to say (Ch20v21) 'If a man shall take his brother's wife, it is an unclean thing.......they shall be childless'. But Papal Dispensation had in fact been obtained. But Henry countered that he had no sons. Queen Catherine had only one living daughter, Mary Tudor. Clearly this was all grotesque and self-serving nonsense from a man who wanted simply another wife to bear him sons. Ordinarily he would have been granted the annulment he sought. But in this case, the Holy Roman Emperor, Charles V, had overrun the Papal States and the Pope, Clement VII, was under Charles' direct control. Charles was the nephew, no less, of Catherine of Aragon herself. He was not going to let his aunt be treated in this way by some jumped up English king. There was now no chance of an annulment being granted. What was Henry now to do?

His faithful minister, Cardinal Wolsey, had not achieved the divorce which Henry had expected him to do, and was sacked. Fortunately, he died before the king could inflict his usual punishment. Henry's new chief minister was Thomas

Cromwell. It was Cromwell who came up with the solution. Why should the English Church still be subject to Papal control? If that authority was granted to the king instead, he could dissolve his own marriage. This was done.

The Act in Restraint of Appeals was passed in 1533. It was a piece of legislation drafted by Cromwell forbidding all appeals to the Pope in Rome on religious or other matters making the English sovereign the final legal authority in his place. The following year, the Act of Supremacy 1534, made the king 'the only supreme head in earth of the Church of England called Anglicana Ecclesia'. This legislation enabled Thomas Cranmer, the Archbishop of Canterbury, to annul Henry's marriage to Catherine of Aragon, so that he could marry the now pregnant Anne Boleyn.

Ironically the Anglican Church, that some of us still love so much, came into being for purely political rather than religious reasons. Apart from the brief restoration of the Roman Catholic Church in the reign of Henry's daughter, Mary I (1553-1558), the Church not 'in England' anymore, but 'of England', has been the established church of the realm of which the monarch is now Supreme Governor rather than Head. A further irony was that poor Anne Boleyn gave birth only to a daughter, Elizabeth. Henry was not to know that she would become one of England's greatest rulers. But, as we all know, Anne never produced the male heir and, since a further annulment was not thought the decent thing to do, the poor woman, who was a bit outspoken to say the least, lost her head on trumped up charges of adultery. It was left to the third wife, Jane Seymour, to produce the male heir, Prince Edward. But she died not long after giving birth. The spare to the heir was still required. For this, and other purely diplomatic reasons, Henry married Anne of Cleves, a German princess. *Fortunately for Anne the king liked neither her smell nor her looks!* The marriage was never consummated and was annulled quickly. Anne enjoyed a quiet and peaceful retirement. The king's eyes then alighted on a young floosy, called Catherine Howard, who became his fifth wife. She might well have provided the spare, but she did commit adultery foolishly with a young courtier. This was treason and, with a king like Henry, the penalty was inevitable and Catherine's head was chopped off. *The job of his sixth and last wife, Katherine Parr, was to look after the now old Henry and tuck him up in bed at night!*

Other than the change of leader there was little else different in the new Church of England. The king had a strong preference for traditional Catholic liturgy and practices. Protestant reformers were unable to make any major changes to the practices of the Church of England. So, both Protestants and Roman Catholics alike were tried for heresy and could be burnt at the stake if convicted. There was one major innovation when, in 1539, 'The Great Bible' was published, the first in English, authorised by King Henry VIII, to be read aloud at Anglican services. The bible was commissioned by Thomas Cromwell and prepared by Myles Coverdale.

Henry's attitude to Church reform was summed up by his views on clerical celibacy. The real Protestant churches on the continent did not see the need for this to continue. Their clergy were marrying increasingly. But Henry still objected to married priests. His own Archbishop of Canterbury, Thomas Cranmer, had long since taken a German wife from Nuremberg, Margarethe. This was anglicised to Margaret. They had two children. But whilst the ban on clerical marriage remained, her existence had to be kept a closely guarded secret. Apparently she was carried around in a coffin-like box with holes in the side, so that she could breathe. At the various Archbishops' Palaces she had to pretend to be a servant. The mind boggles at this extraordinary state of affairs. So, this farce had to carry on until Henry died. Cranmer was to be the major force in the English reformation that took place in the reign of Henry's son, Edward VI.

Before I move on to Edward there is one major matter I must mention. As I have pointed out previously monastic life had existed from before the Norman conquest and continued to flourish ever afterwards. The monasteries were major religious, educational and cultural centres whose contribution to the development of England was a great, almost entirely beneficial one. It was true that, by the 16th century, some degree of corruption had tarnished monastic life. The same fraudulent practices, in relation to indulgences and so-called holy relics, *remember my nose*, had, to a certain extent, appeared. The monasteries could have been reformed easily, if it had been desired to do so. But the monasteries were, by and large, wealthy institutions. The Crown was always looking for extra cash. Henry VIII and his henchman, Thomas Cromwell, took now full advantage of the break with Rome to confiscate the wealth of the monasteries and to destroy utterly their buildings. This took place largely between 1536 and 1540. This brought to an end a major part of English life. *It was, without doubt, the biggest act of cultural vandalism ever witnessed by this country. The ruins of these once great buildings still litter our land. Of all King Henry's crimes and, there were many, I cannot help thinking this was his most heinous.*

The English Reformation

King Henry VIII died at the beginning of 1547 and was succeeded by his 9-year-old son, Edward, who became King Edward VI. He was too young to rule in person, but he was an exceptionally intelligent boy, who might have become a truly great king had he not died so tragically young, aged only 15, in 1553. By the time of his death he was exerting already increasing influence over all matters including Church reform. Thomas Cranmer was a committed Protestant and the driving force behind the English Reformation, which could proceed now that Henry VIII was out of the way.

I assume that poor old Margaret Cranmer was released from her box, at least from 1549, when clerical marriage was legalised. Protestant churches do not see the need for clerical celibacy. It had never been enforced universally throughout the history of the Roman Catholic Church. Some of the apostles such as Peter were married. How can a priest minister properly to the needs of his flock if he has no knowledge of how family life works? Fundamentally there is nothing in the scriptures to say that priests should not marry. The Canon Law of the Church of England allows now Priests and Bishops of the Church of England to marry 'as they shall judge the same to serve better to godliness'. Clergymen may be married or single, as best suits their calling.

Cranmer believed firmly in a new Church liturgy in English. He was responsible for and introduced a new Book of Common Prayer in 1549, written in the vernacular. It was given legal force by the Act of Uniformity 1549. Its use was compulsory. The Archbishop now revealed that he was opposed to the Roman Catholic doctrine of transubstantiation and believed that the presence of Jesus Christ in the Eucharist was spiritual only. The majority of the population remained loyal still to the old faith.

Then Cranmer published the Ordinal in 1550, which was the liturgy for the ordination of priests. It created three services for ordaining bishops, priests and deacons. In the same year Cranmer produced the Defence of the True and Catholic Doctrine of the Sacrament of the Body and Blood of Christ. It is an explanation of the eucharistic theology within the new Prayer Book. In the preface Cranmer summarises his quarrel with Rome when he compares 'beads, pardons, pilgrimages, and such other like popery' with weeds. The roots of the weeds are transubstantiation, the doctrine of the Real Presence and the sacrificial nature of the mass.

In today's Anglican Church the attitude towards transubstantiation differs reflecting the all-embracing, but frequently infuriating, nature of its tradition. Most Evangelicals take the view that the sacrament is simply a memorial of Christ's death and passion; a memorial of Christ's suffering and participation in the eucharist, as both a re-enactment of the Last Supper and a foreshadowing of the heavenly banquet where the eucharistic promise is fulfilled. Anglo-Catholics, on the other hand, tend to go the whole hog and subscribe to the Roman Church's doctrine of transubstantiation with the eucharistic elements actually transformed into Christ's body and blood. Mainstream Anglicans tend to believe in a bit of both naturally. Certainly, when the whole issue is looked at closely it does become something of the 'How many angels can dance on the end of a pinhead?' variety. When it comes down to it, what is the difference between the actual physical presence of Jesus Christ in the eucharist and his spiritual presence only? Some would say that it is fundamental, but I am not so sure. When I come to say something about the reign of Elizabeth I, I hope you will see why the whole argument has become so convoluted.

After the publication of the first revised Book of Common Prayer, Cranmer then worked on a further revision of the Prayer Book and the formation of a statement of doctrine. He attempted also to revise canon law, given the break with Rome, but, due to political disputes, the revisions never passed through Parliament. The further revision of the Prayer Book began in late 1550. The belief that Christ was present in the eucharist in a spiritual way only was emphasised by the use of entirely different words when communicants were offered the bread and the wine. New rubrics noted that any form of bread could be used and that, any bread or wine that remained, could be used by the celebrant. Thus, the elements of the sacrament were divorced from any physical presence. Prayers for the dead were prohibited as they implied support for the Roman Catholic doctrine of purgatory. The Act of Uniformity 1552, authorising the book's use, specified that it be used exclusively from 1st November. But, in practical terms, implementation of the revised Prayer Book was delayed substantially and had made little impact by the time of King Edward's death in July 1553.

The origins of the Statement of Doctrine which became the Forty-Two Articles are somewhat obscure. As early as December 1549, the Archbishop was demanding from his bishops subscription to certain doctrinal articles. In 1551 Cranmer presented a version of a statement to the bishops, but its status remained ambiguous. But, like the revised Prayer Book, implementation of the Articles was prevented by the king's death and everything was thrown into turmoil under the reign of his successor, Mary I. Nevertheless, the Books of Common Prayer and the articles of religion, as revised, still remain the basis of Church of England belief today.

The practical aspect of the reformation in Edward's reign was the destruction of all religious art and other iconography in our cathedrals and churches, which were now regarded as Romish idolatry. Again, much of this seems now a pointless waste and it is in only a few medieval places of worship today that one can see the fine murals that once adorned their walls. The great medieval frontages of Lincoln and Wells Cathedral were, in their heyday, decorated with the brightly painted statues of the saints. The statues remain, but the decoration no more alas.

The Catholic Counter-Reformation under Queen Mary I

1553 brought a temporary end to the English Reformation. Young King Edward became ill. Whilst the precise nature of the disease was not known at the time it is thought now that it was almost certainly tuberculosis. Edward was not going to recover and he had no heirs. Under the terms of Henry VIII's will the crown was to pass, in this eventuality, to his eldest daughter, Mary Tudor, his child by Catherine of Aragon and Edward's half-sister. This raised an alarming prospect for the Protestant reformers. Mary Tudor was a devout Roman Catholic. Like all her family she was a very intelligent woman. But she was intensely bitter at the way both she and her mother had been treated as a result of the break with Rome. She was determined to restore the Roman Catholic faith to England when Edward died and she became Queen in her own right, the first woman to do so. The senior Protestants in the government made a failed attempt to stop this by putting the tragic figure of Lady Jane Grey, 'The Nine Days Queen' on the throne when Edward died; she was both of royal blood and a Protestant. But the people recognised the true Queen as Mary and she was crowned Queen of England on 1st October 1553.

It was not long before leading Protestant churchmen, including Thomas Cranmer himself, Hugh Latimer, Bishop of Worcester and Nicholas Ridley, Bishop of London, were imprisoned. Mary's first Parliament declared the marriage of her parents valid and abolished King Edward's religious laws. Church doctrine was restored to the form it had been before the death of King Henry VIII in 1547. Transubstantiation and clerical celibacy were both restored. Married priests were deprived of their benefices. Parliament repealed subsequently the laws enacting the break with Rome and the authority of the Pope was thus restored. But Mary and Pope Julius III had to accept that the monastic lands, confiscated by Henry VIII, must remain in the hands of their new owners to avoid the risk of domestic rebellion.

Mary revived the Heresy Acts under which numerous Protestants were executed. The first executions occurred over a period of five days in early February 1555. Bishops Latimer and Ridley were burnt at the stake in October of that year. Thomas Cranmer was forced to watch. Afterwards, Cranmer decided to repudiate Protestantism and rejoined the Catholic faith. But Mary refused to commute the death sentence, probably because of the role Cranmer had played in the dissolution of her mother's marriage. On the day of his execution in March 1556, when the fire was lit, the Archbishop re-affirmed his Protestant faith and thrust famously his right hand, with which he had signed his cowardly recantation, into the fire first. In the whole of Mary's reign there were about 280 Protestant martyrs. Mary earned the soubriquet 'Bloody Mary'. Religious persecution and war have been a terrible indictment of many who have preached supposedly in the name of Christ. On Cranmer's execution Cardinal Reginald Pole, a man of royal descent from the Plantagenets, became the new Roman Catholic, Archbishop of Canterbury.

But all was not lost for the Protestant cause. Whilst the majority of the ordinary population may have been loyal to the old faith many powerful members of the establishment were not. The restored faith was only likely to survive if Mary had a Catholic heir to succeed her. But in 1553, when Mary came to the throne, she was a woman who was unmarried and not far off 40 years of age. She married quickly a man, over 10 years her junior, Prince Philip of Spain, the heir to his father, the King of Spain and Holy Roman Emperor, Charles V. He became King consort of England. Mary was impressed with her catch. Philip was not quite so keen. But Mary did become pregnant apparently, but, when her pregnancy went considerably beyond the usual term, it became clear rapidly that this was a 'phantom' pregnancy. Tragically, in 1558, Mary thought she was pregnant again, but, in fact, it was not conception that had occurred, but the onset of cancer. Mary and Cardinal Pole both died on 17th November 1558. Mary's only heir was her younger Protestant half-sister, Elizabeth, the daughter of Anne Boleyn, who became Queen Elizabeth I of England.

CARDINAL REGINALD POLE
THE MOST FAMOUS CARDINAL THAT EVER LIVED!

I must tell the story of the great Cardinal Pole, a man truly famous throughout the world or so my father thought! Our family and, maybe yours, played a silly parlour game at Christmas and other similar times called 'Who am I?'. All each player had to do was to pretend to be a famous person from history, politics, sport or whatever. The other players then ask a series of questions to identify the person concerned. It usually proves to be not that difficult as people tend to choose personalities that they know something about and that is almost always a strong clue as to where the identity of the person lies. On one occasion my dear father chose to be Cardinal Pole of all people. Certainly, a person from an ecclesiastical background, but neither I, at that stage, nor any other family members, who have no interest in history, ecclesiastical or otherwise, had ever heard of him! Needless to say, my father won his round. When he revealed that he was Cardinal Pole this caused a storm of protest about picking unidentifiable characters. My sister's husband cried 'foul'! My father could not understand why nobody, not even his history-loving son, James, had ever heard of the eminent cardinal, the last Roman Catholic Archbishop of Canterbury! He simply looked hurt, misunderstood and nonplussed at his family's ignorance. I sometimes now wonder whether, in fact, he chose the character deliberately to win the round and to have a good, inward laugh at what he had done. Whenever the game was next played Cardinal Pole became a running joke in relation to who my dear father would be next. A reminder of happy family times. I doubt that, sadly, any other members of my family would remember this story at all now. They are all too transfixed by more important things. Well, it is sometimes the trivial that brightens up life, I think.

The Protestant Restoration under Queen Elizabeth I

Immediately the Act of Supremacy 1558 re-established the Church of England's independence from Rome. Elizabeth became the Supreme Governor of the Church of England. *Not 'Head' as women were not thought able to act in this role; they must have been very stupid men who made this decision as any married man knows today!* The Act of Uniformity 1559 re-introduced the 1552 Book of Common Prayer (BCP), which contained the liturgical services of the Church and was modified in 1559 to allow a more liberal attitude towards the Catholic doctrine of the Real Presence. The BCP became the yardstick of Anglicanism, which came to see its identity mainly in liturgy and institutional continuity and, to a lesser extent, in what became now the Thirty-Nine Articles of Religion, which sought to navigate a middle way (*via media*) between Roman Catholicism, Continental Protestantism and radical sects.

Whilst Queen Elizabeth was a Protestant, she realised that both her ecclesiastical and lay nobility, as well as the common people, were divided strongly between the old and new faiths. She wished to introduce a Church which, so far as was possible, would be acceptable to both religious traditions which is why the Anglican Church is such a curious mixture to this day; neither wholly Protestant nor wholly Catholic. Frequently it is a mass of inherent contradictions.

Thomas Cranmer was influenced mainly by Calvinism. John Calvin's main mentor, the German, Martin Bucer, fled to England in 1548. Whilst he died less than a year later, he had been in touch with Cranmer for many years and his influence can be seen clearly in the Thirty-Nine Articles. Cranmer came to reject the idea that good works alone might lead to salvation. He believed in the new Protestant doctrine of 'Justification by Faith'. Bucer and Cranmer corresponded also about the doctrine of transubstantiation, which the German made clear he rejected entirely. The Articles of Religion are influenced by Calvinist thought. Generally, Article VI and Articles XI to XIV deal with the question of Justification by Faith. Article XXVIII condemns the doctrine of the Real Presence. Article XXXII permits the marriage of priests. The authority of the Pope, the 'Bishop of Rome', is rejected.

Queen Elizabeth herself inclined towards the doctrine of the Real Presence. The 1559 Prayer Book took a far more liberal line on this issue, catering for what the sovereign wanted. To this day the Anglican Church (the term Anglican started being used towards the end of the 16th century) consists of three wings; the Low Church, Protestant, Evangelical wing, the Anglo-Catholic, High Church wing and the Broad Church, middle of the road wing. This is what gives the Church of England its truly distinct flavour. The Elizabethan settlement allowed also the continuing use of a substantial degree of ceremony of one kind or another. In today's Low Church wing one will find almost none. In the High Church wing one will find the lavish use of candles, colourful vestments, incense and the like, possibly more Catholic than the Roman Catholics themselves. The Broad Church tradition, to which I adhere, is a mixture of some ceremony rather than none. Some priests will wear vestments, although I never did myself. *I did possess a very fine, ceremonial blue and cream cope, which I enjoyed thoroughly putting on for processions round the church and for the great festivals of Christmas, Easter and Whitsun.* The choir was fully robed and surpliced to sing the services; the great choral Sung Eucharists and choral Matins of my own times. That tradition was destroyed by the 'fools' of the late 1960s onwards.

If I was pressed I would say always that I leaned towards the Catholic rather than Protestant tradition. I think the Anglican Church is best summed up by these maybe slightly familiar words:-

> *"When they were high, they were high*
> *And when they were low, they were low*
> *And when they were only halfway high*
> *They were neither high nor low".*

Now we shall see soon that, this apparent catering to the needs of all, gave rise in the 17th century to the most savage divisions in the Anglican Church, between Low Church puritans and High Church Anglo-Catholics.

Father and Mother on their wedding day, August 23rd 1947

St Mary's Church

St Mary's Rectory (Lambeth Palace)

The Village Shop (sellers of the 'Love Pill')

Harsnetts (The Vatican)

Father and Mother on the occasion of their fortieth wedding anniversary,
August 23rd 1987

Father with the monster 'George' before his journey to the vet for despatch to Heaven above or Hell below!

The author with Sally and Father

AUGUST

THE FIRST HALF OF THE 17ᵀᴴ CENTURY: TRIUMPH AND DISASTER

In 1603 Queen Elizabeth I died. The Tudor dynasty was a truly formidable family. Their one major weakness was lack of fertility. Henry VIII had provided only one short-lived son. His daughters, Mary and Elizabeth, had no children at all. The Tudor dynasty died out. The English throne passed to Elizabeth's Scottish cousin, King James VI of Scotland, a direct descendant of Margaret Tudor, Henry VIII's elder sister, who had married King James IV of Scotland. The mother of James VI had been the ill-fated Mary Queen of Scots, a devout Roman Catholic. After her ill-advised flight to England she was executed after 18 years' imprisonment. Her infant son had succeeded to the Scottish throne and had been brought up a Protestant. He was a member of the Scottish Presbyterian Church, the Kirk. He was thus a totally acceptable heir to Elizabeth and became King James I of England.

Whilst James was a Presbyterian, he came to lean increasingly towards the Church of England, since Anglicanism favoured wholly the episcopacy, which the Kirk did not. In Elizabeth's time, whilst she sought a religious policy acceptable to as many of her people as possible, devout Roman Catholics did not accept her compromise. The Crown passed laws requiring everyone to attend Anglican Church services. Those who did not, called recusants, were subject to heavy fines. Most Roman Catholics made the minimum attendance necessary to avoid the penalties. Some did not. Others continued to hear Mass in their own homes and Catholic priests were brought in to celebrate the Mass illegally. This led to the famous 'priest-holes' to hide the whereabouts of priests. Those Roman Catholic priests captured were tortured and put to death frequently. Now that James had come to the throne Roman Catholics hoped that the laws would be relaxed. Why is not totally clear. Perhaps because James' mother had been such a loyal member of the old faith. What they failed to recognise was that James had not been influenced by his mother at all. The laws were not eased, giving rise to the famous 'Gunpowder Plot' of 1605 to blow up Parliament with the new king and the entire Protestant establishment in it. When the plot failed the laws against Roman Catholics were tightened up and were not relaxed substantially until Catholic emancipation in 1829. As a gesture to Roman Catholic opinion James did, about ten years later, have the remains of his mother moved from Peterborough Cathedral to their current resting-place in the King Henry VII Chapel at Westminster Abbey.

Triumph

In 1604 King James called the Hampton Court conference of senior churchmen, which requested that the English Bible be revised because existing translations 'were corrupt and not answerable to the truth of the original.' King Henry VIII's Bible, known as 'The Great Bible', enjoyed some popularity, but successive editions exhibited a number of inconsistencies. The Bishops' Bible of 1568 was well regarded by the clergy, but failed to gain wide acceptance or the official authorisation of Elizabeth. The most popular English translation was the Geneva Bible of 1557, first published in England in 1576. It had been prepared by English Protestants living in Geneva during Mary Tudor's persecutions. This Bible was not approved by the Crown but it was popular amongst puritans.

Since the need for a new authorised translation was recognised widely, King James was quick to adopt the project as his own. By June 30th 1604 James had approved a list of 54 revisers, although records show that only 47 scholars actually participated. They were organised into six groups. The Archbishop of Canterbury, Richard Bancroft (1544–1610), served as overseer and established doctrinal conventions for the translators. The new Bible was published in 1611.

The translation of the Bible was undertaken, under royal sponsorship, on a vast scale. An elaborate set of rules was put together to curb individual prejudices and to ensure the translation's scholarly and non-partisan character. In contrast to earlier practice, the new version was to use vulgar forms of proper names. For example, 'Jonas' or 'Jonah' for the Hebrew 'Yonah', in keeping with its aim to make the Scriptures popular and familiar. The translators used the original Greek and Hebrew texts. They used also the existing English-language translations, including the partial translation made by William Tyndale (c.1490–1536), and also Jewish commentaries to guide their work. The wealth of scholarly material, available to the translators, made their translation a great exercise in originality and independent judgment. For this reason, the new version is more faithful to the original languages of the Bible and more scholarly than any of its predecessors. The impact of the original Hebrew upon the revisers is so pronounced that they seem to have made a conscious effort to imitate its rhythm and style in their translation of the Hebrew Scriptures. The literary style of the translation of the New Testament, some say, is actually superior to that of the Greek original. *Some errors in further editions became famous. For instance, the so-called 'Wicked Bible' of 1631, whose name derives from the omission of 'not' in the commandment against adultery: 'Thou shalt commit adultery!'. The printers were fined £300 for the error, a large sum of money for the time.*

From the time of publication, the Authorised Version has been the standard translation throughout the Anglican Communion and elsewhere. The King James Bible was written by some great men of the Christian faith. Their many arguments and disputes enabled them to produce a form of the Bible which many people regarded and regard still as almost divinely inspired. Even those who profess no faith see the Authorised Version as one of the three great works of the English language, together with the 'Complete Works of Shakespeare' and 'The Book of Common Prayer' of 1662. But it is as a Bible that it should be judged and not simply as a work of literature, although the quality of the language contributes hugely to its spiritual value.

It was this great Bible that persisted in use right down to the 1960s. As with liturgical reform the 'fools' intervened. In the face of dwindling Church congregations, the 'fools' decided that, as regards the Bible, ordinary people could not understand it. They made the same decision in relation to the Church's liturgy. A modern translation of the Bible and a modern liturgy would bring people back to the Church. Well, to say this has not happened, is the proverbial understatement.

Numerous modern translations of the Bible have been produced now. I do not say that they are all without any merit. My own favourite modern translation is 'The Good News Bible' which I think matches the spirit of King James the best. I think there are circumstances where to use a modern translation may very well be helpful to some people.

What I think is scandalous is that the King James Bible has been all but eliminated from normal Anglican Church parish use. The Church of England caters now for all kinds of different tastes and usages. What it does not provide is even an occasional spot for the Authorised Version.

I am going to compare and contrast a number of well-known passages in the Bible. I will use both the Authorised Version and, my preferred modern version, 'The Good News Bible'. I do not ask you to say which one is best. No doubt you will have your own views. But is the Authorised Version really that difficult to understand? I think not at all. At least I hope its beauty still shines through.

The first extract is from the famous Prologue to the Gospel of St John 1 vvs1-14 dealing with Jesus, the 'Word made flesh' who 'dwelt' among us.

Authorised Version	Good News Bible
1 In the beginning was the Word, and the Word was with God, and the Word was God.	1 In the beginning the Word already existed; the Word was with God, and the Word was God.
2 The same was in the beginning with God.	2 From the very beginning the Word was with God.
3 All things were made by him; and without him was not any thing made that was made.	3 Through him God made all things; not one thing in all creation was made without him.
4 In him was life; and the life was the light of men.	4 The Word was the source of life,and this life brought light to people.
5 And the light shineth in darkness; and the darkness comprehended it not.	5 The light shines in the darkness, and the darkness has never put it out.
6 There was a man sent from God, whose name *was* John.	6 God sent his messenger, a man named John,
7 The same came for a witness, to bear witness of the Light, that all *men* through him might believe.	7 who came to tell people about the light, so that all should hear the message and believe.
8 He was not that Light, but *was sent* to bear witness of that Light.	8 He himself was not the light; he came to tell about the light.
9 *That* was the true Light, which lighteth every man that cometh into the world.	9 This was the real light - the light that comes into the world and shines on all people.
10 He was in the world, and the world was made by him, and the world knew him not.	10 The Word was in the world, and though God made the world through him, yet the world did not recognize him.
11 He came unto his own, and his own received him not.	11 He came to his own country, but his own people did not receive him.
12 But as many as received him, to them gave he power to become the sons of God, *even* to them that believe on his name:	12 Some, however, did receive him and believed in him; so he gave them the right to become God's children.
13 Which were born, not of blood, nor of the will of the flesh, nor of the will of man, but of God.	13 They did not become God's children by natural means, that is, by being born as the children of a human father; God himself was their Father.
14 And the Word was made flesh, and dwelt among us, (and we beheld his glory, the glory as of the only begotten of the Father,) full of grace and truth.	14 The Word became a human being and, full of grace and truth, lived among us. We saw his glory, the glory which he received as the Father's only Son.

The second extract is the nativity story from St Luke Ch2vvs8-16.

Authorised Version	Good News Bible
8 And there were in the same country shepherds abiding in the field, keeping watch over their flock by night.	**8** There were some shepherds in that part of the country who were spending the night in the fields, taking care of their flocks.
9 And, lo, the angel of the Lord came upon them, and the glory of the Lord shone round about them: and they were sore afraid.	**9** An angel of the Lord appeared to them, and the glory of the Lord shone over them. They were terribly afraid,
10 And the angel said unto them, Fear not: for, behold, I bring you good tidings of great joy, which shall be to all people.	**10** but the angel said to them, 'Don't be afraid! I am here with good news for you, which will bring great joy to all the people.
11 For unto you is born this day in the city of David a Saviour, which is Christ the Lord.	**11** This very day in David's town your Saviour was born - Christ the Lord!
12 And this shall be a sign unto you; Ye shall find the babe wrapped in swaddling clothes, lying in a manger.	**12** And this is what will prove it to you: you will find a baby wrapped in cloths and lying in a manger.'
13 And suddenly there was with the angel a multitude of the heavenly host praising God, and saying,	**13** Suddenly a great army of heaven's angels appeared with the angel, singing praises to God:
14 Glory to God in the highest, and on earth peace, good will toward men.	**14** 'Glory to God in the highest heaven, and peace on earth to those with whom he is pleased!'
15 And it came to pass, as the angels were gone away from them into heaven, the shepherds said one to another, Let us now go even unto Bethlehem, and see this thing which is come to pass, which the Lord hath made known unto us.	**15** When the angels went away from them back into heaven, the shepherds said to one another, 'Let's go to Bethlehem and see this thing that has happened, which the Lord has told us.'
16 And they came with haste, and found Mary, and Joseph, and the babe lying in a manger.	**16** So they hurried off and found Mary and Joseph and saw the baby lying in the manger.

The third extract is the resurrection story from St John Ch20vv1-18

Authorised Version	Good News Bible
1 The first day of the week cometh Mary Magdalene early, when it was yet dark, unto the sepulchre, and seeth the stone taken away from the sepulchre.	1 Early on Sunday morning, while it was still dark, Mary Magdalene went to the tomb and saw that the stone had been taken away from the entrance.
2 Then she runneth, and cometh to Simon Peter, and to the other disciple, whom Jesus loved, and saith unto them, They have taken away the Lord out of the sepulchre, and we know not where they have laid him.	2 She went running to Simon Peter and the other disciple, whom Jesus loved, and told them, 'They have taken the Lord from the tomb, and we don't know where they have put him!'
3 Peter therefore went forth,and that other disciple, and came to the sepulchre.	3 Then Peter and the other disciple went to the tomb.
4 So they ran both together: and the other disciple did outrun Peter, and came first to the sepulchre.	4 The two of them were running, but the other disciple ran faster than Peter and reached the tomb first.
5 And he stooping down, and looking in, saw the linen clothes lying; yet went he not in.	5 He bent over and saw the linen cloths, but he did not go in.
6 Then cometh Simon Peter following him, and went into the sepulchre, and seeth the linen clothes lie,	6 Behind him came Simon Peter, and he went straight into the tomb. He saw the linen cloths lying there
7 And the napkin, that was about his head, not lying with the linen clothes, but wrapped together in a place by itself.	7 and the cloth which had been around Jesus' head. It was not lying with the linen cloths but was rolled up by itself.
8 Then went in also that other disciple, which came first to the sepulchre, and he saw, and believed.	8 Then the other disciple, who had reached the tomb first, also went in; he saw and believed
9 For as yet they knew not the scripture, that he must rise again from the dead.	9 (They still did not understand the scripture which said that he must rise from death.)
10 Then the disciples went away again unto their own home.	10 Then the disciples went back home.

11 But Mary stood without at the sepulchre weeping: and as she wept, she stooped down, and looked into the sepulchre,

12 And seeth two angels in white sitting, the one at the head, and the other at the feet, where the body of Jesus had lain.

13 And they say unto her, Woman, why weepest thou? She saith unto them, Because they have taken away my Lord, and I know not where they have laid him.

14 And when she had thus said, she turned herself back, and saw Jesus standing, and knew not that it was Jesus.

15 Jesus saith unto her, Woman, why weepest thou? whom seekest thou? She, supposing him to be the gardener, saith unto him, Sir, if thou have borne him hence, tell me where thou hast laid him, and I will take him away.

16 Jesus saith unto her, Mary. She turned herself, and saith unto him, Rabboni; which is to say, Master.

17 Jesus saith unto her, Touch me not; for I am not yet ascended to my Father: but go to my brethren, and say unto them, I ascend unto my Father, and your Father; and to my God, and your God.

18 Mary Magdalene came and told the disciples that she had seen the Lord, and that he had spoken these things unto her.

11 Mary stood crying outside the tomb. While she was still crying, she bent over and looked in the tomb

12 and saw two angels there dressed in white, sitting where the body of Jesus had been, one at the head and the other at the feet.

13 'Woman, why are you crying?' they asked her. She answered, 'They have taken my Lord away, and I do not know where they have put him!'

14 Then she turned around and saw Jesus standing there; but she did not know that it was Jesus.

15 'Woman, why are you crying?' Jesus asked her. 'Who is it that you are looking for?' She thought he was the gardener, so she said to him, 'If you took him away, sir, tell me where you have put him, and I will go and get him.'

16 Jesus said to her, 'Mary!' She turned toward him and said in Hebrew, 'Rabboni!' (This means 'Teacher.')

17 'Do not hold on to me,' Jesus told her, 'because I have not yet gone back up to the Father. But go to my brothers and tell them that I am returning to him who is my Father and their Father, my God and their God.'

18 So Mary Magdalene went and told the disciples that she had seen the Lord and related to them what he had told her.

I think the Good News translation is also a fine one. What I think is that the Church of England should find a use for both old and modern translations. When theatre-goers see a Shakespeare production I doubt they are expecting one in modern English. Remember that the Authorised Version and Shakespeare were both written about the same time. I have not heard it suggested that we should dismiss our greatest playwright. Certainly our cousins across the Atlantic would not. A majority of Americans, whether Episcopalians (Anglicans) or other denominations, still prefer the King James Bible. My increasing experience is that Americans are extremely capable, whether it be in business, cultural or religious matters. We are the fools. *This is, despite what I said once from the pulpit, in front of my own son-in-law, an American by birth: 'Can no good thing come out of America?'*

Disaster

King James I was a strange man. He was said to be 'The Wisest Fool in Christendom'. This was due apparently to his buffoonish behaviour, which was at variance with the fact that he was an intensely learned man. He wrote a number of highly intellectual discourses on the 'Divine Right of Kings'. I think the nature of this somewhat dubious concept contributed to his soubriquet. But, in fact, James was a wily old fox who, despite the pomposities of his writings, recognised that he had to keep both Parliament and important people on his side if he was to rule effectively. But in 1625 James died and was succeeded by his second son, Charles I, who was to prove a true fool in virtually every respect, although not in the sense I mean it today.

Charles was certainly not a bad man personally. He loved his wife and children unlike a good many of his fellow rulers. He was a faithful son of the Catholic wing of the

Church of England. But he was a quite hopeless politician. He believed genuinely that he was God's duly appointed representative on earth and that he had the right to rule absolutely. This was complete codswallop. Even in Medieval times monarchs either lost or came close to losing their thrones due to incompetent rule. Remember King John, King Henry III, King Edward II, King Richard II and King Henry VI; not to mention King Richard III who, whilst not perhaps incompetent, was deemed otherwise unfit to rule. It was not long before Charles got into substantial trouble with Parliament over the raising of taxation. It had been established for centuries that all new or additional taxation required the approval of Parliament. But Charles was unable to obtain approval for the taxation he needed to become involved in the wars of religion then devastating Europe. On 26th May 1628 Parliament adopted a Petition of Right, calling upon the king to acknowledge that he could not levy taxes without Parliament's consent, that he could not impose martial law on civilians, that he could not imprison them without due process of law and that he could not quarter troops in their homes. Charles assented to the Petition on 7th June but, by the end of the month, he had prorogued Parliament and re-asserted his right to collect customs duties without authorisation from Parliament. The following year he dissolved Parliament, following further opposition to his taxation policies and his Catholic approach to religion. For the next eleven years Charles ruled England, without Parliament, relying on customs-duties and other devices, such as the notorious ship money, to provide the revenue which he could raise under the royal prerogative without reference to Parliament. Against a background of general prosperity this worked well.

William Laud was appointed Archbishop of Canterbury in 1633 during the period of Charles' personal rule. He was a significant religious and political advisor. During his time as the Archbishop of Canterbury Laud attempted to impose order and unity on the Church of England through the implementation of a series of religious reforms. These attacked the strict Protestant practices of the Low Church wing of the Church of England, the English Puritans. They, in turn, accused him of popery, tyranny and treason. He is considered now one of the leading instigators of the conflict between Crown and Parliament, which ended in the English Civil War.

The Church became more and more Calvinist in doctrine in the latter stages of the reign of Elizabeth I and that of James I. This corresponded with the increasing number of Puritans in England. Laud reacted by criticising this development; Church dogma had become too Calvinist and services too stern. Laud found backing in his quest for reform from the King and prominent noblemen. They supported Arminianism, a strand of Protestantism that rejected some of the key Calvinist doctrines, such as predestination, and instead focussed on the belief that salvation could be achieved through free will. The reform led to increasing tension between the Archbishop and the laity.

One of Laud's most controversial actions was to restore church ceremony and interior decoration to reflect the aesthetic grandeur of the pre-Reformation church. This was reflected in the re-introduction of traditional clergy vestments, images and stained-glass windows in churches and cathedrals to reflect the divinity of God's presence on earth. The most controversial issue was when Laud ordered that the communion table should be made out of stone, not wood, and had to be placed against the east wall of the chancel, surrounded by railings. *This remains the practice largely to this day, although some churches now prefer a more central positioning of the altar.* Thus, the laity had to kneel at the rails in order to receive communion. The Puritans considered the changes were too similar to the Roman Catholic Mass, and protests against the Archbishop's order occurred immediately.

Laud arranged inspections of parish churches to enforce these changes and punish non-conformists. The inspections were intrusive and ensured that all aspects of his aesthetic and doctrinal policies were in place. Laud's persistent attack on non-conformists was intensified in 1637 when the Puritan writers, William Prynne, Henry Burton and John Bastwick were sentenced to have their ears removed and cheeks branded after publishing writings against Laud. This was considered a shocking and unnecessary punishment, which accentuated the resentment Protestants felt towards Laud and the Church. It created Puritan martyrs out of the victims.

Clearly the king, a high churchman himself, had approved all these changes. The fatal error of both the king and Laud was when they attempted to impose the Anglican Book of Common Prayer in 1637 on the Presbyterian Kirk, the established church of Scotland. When a service using the new Prayer Book began at St Giles' Cathedral in Edinburgh it resulted in a wholesale riot. It led to the National Covenant of 1638 when the Scots attacked the Pope, the episcopate generally and the introduction of the new Prayer Book in particular. By 1639 war with Scotland appeared increasingly likely. King Charles had insufficient resources for such a conflict and he was forced to call Parliament, for the first time in eleven years, in order to secure additional taxation.

The initial 'Short Parliament' of 1640 was dissolved after less than two months when Parliament refused taxation until the king dealt with their grievances. Later that year Charles had to recall the Parliament, which has become known to history as the 'Long Parliament'. It sat right through until dismissed by Oliver Cromwell in 1653 and was recalled then briefly before the restoration of the monarchy in 1660. The House of Commons had a majority of Puritan supporters and others who were determined again that the king should have no further money until reform had been granted. This Charles was not prepared to do. The descent to all-out civil war between the king and Parliament was both steep and swift. By the autumn of 1642 Charles had left London and he raised the royal standard at Nottingham declaring war on Parliament. Following the Battle of Naseby in 1645 the king had been defeated completely and was imprisoned.

Charles, being the foolish man that he was, conspired then in secret with the Scots, now his friends again, giving rise to the second civil war in which his cause was crushed far more quickly than the first. Whilst Parliament had been prepared previously to allow the monarchy to continue it felt now that Charles had to be removed for good. He was convicted of treason against his own people and beheaded on 30th January 1649. High Church Anglicans saw the king's execution as a martyrdom and the observance remained part of the Book of Common Prayer until 1859. Some Anglo-Catholics retain the tradition to this day, most notably, the Society of King Charles the Martyr. Martyr or not he was, to my mind, even though I am personally a devoted monarchist, a very stupid man, whose actions led to the abolition of the monarchy and this country's first and only republic in 1649.

So, what was the effect of all this on the Church of England? Effectively it ceased to exist. After the recall of Parliament in 1640 there were mass demonstrations against Archbishop Laud who was accused of treason. King Charles felt he had no option but to allow his Archbishop to be imprisoned. He remained there until 1644. Whilst many hoped that Laud, a man now over 70, would be allowed to die in prison, he was tried and convicted of treason that year and beheaded on Tower Hill. A replacement was not appointed until the restoration of the monarchy in 1660. The Anglican Church was not abolished formally, but its bishops and priests retreated largely into obscurity.

THE SECOND HALF OF THE 17TH CENTURY: RESTORATION AND ZENITH

The English Republic, better known as the Commonwealth, lasted until the restoration of the monarchy in 1660. *The Commonwealth was ruled by that frightful man, Oliver Cromwell. My son, James, tries always to tell me that Cromwell was an effective ruler, warts and all, and that he was not just the spoilsport who banned Christmas celebrations. But he would have prevented me from playing my favourite parlour game 'Who am I?'. That is enough to damn him for me! The wart died in 1658 and no effective successor could be found.*

So, the English people decided to restore the monarchy in the person of Charles I's eldest son, Charles II, who had spent most of the Commonwealth period as an exile on the continent. Charles II made a triumphal return to London in May 1660. He was as unlike his father as it was possible to be. He was tall and good looking. He was a total ladies' man incapable of marital fidelity. He had numerous mistresses throughout his reign, the best known of whom was Nell Gwynne. He sired umpteen illegitimate children. Unfortunately, his wife, Catherine of Braganza, proved barren and no direct heirs to the throne were produced. This led to great problems later on. Charles' court was seen as louche and debauched as it was possible to be. Charles was not a particularly good ruler but, unlike his father and more like his grandfather, he was politically astute enough never to put his hold on the throne in any real danger. He wished famously 'never to have to go on his travels again'. But in religious terms he was like his father. He was a high churchman. But, unlike his father again, Charles was attracted to the Roman Catholic Church. He knew that it would be impossible politically to join that Church in his lifetime, but, on his deathbed in 1685, he was received into the Church of Rome.

Both Crown and Church of England were restored largely to the same position as they had been before the civil war. Church and state were at one together again. Charles II appointed William Juxon as Archbishop of Canterbury. He was the man who had acted as Charles I's chaplain before his execution in 1649.

The Book of Common Prayer 1662

The victory of the Parliamentarians in the civil wars had resulted in the banning of the Books of Common Prayer under the Commonwealth and Protectorate. The restored Church decided now to revise and publish a new Book of Common Prayer. Many English Presbyterians had helped the king's restoration and they hoped that some concessions would be made to their views. The 1662 Prayer Book was printed only two years after the restoration of the monarchy, following the Savoy Conference, between representatives of the Presbyterian Church and twelve bishops. There, the Presbyterians urged the omission of such ceremonies as making the sign of the Cross in Baptism, and wanted the use of the surplice to be optional, and permission either to sit or to kneel at the Holy Communion. A major concession to some of the requests of the Presbyterians would no doubt have kept many of them from seceding from the Anglican Church, but both sides were unreasonable thus preventing anything in the way of a compromise. The ideal of a Church embracing all the people of England was abandoned. The Church of England occupied the middle ground and those Puritans and Protestants who dissented from the Anglican establishment had to continue their existence from outside rather than trying to gain influence from within. The Test Acts, which were passed during the reign of Charles II, excluded from public office both Roman Catholics and the Protestants who were part of the Protestant churches outside the Church of England.

The Savoy Conference ended in disagreement late in July 1661 and the issue of prayer book revision passed to the Church Convocations of Canterbury and York and from there to Parliament. The Book of Common Prayer 1662 is the third great work of the English language. It is only a slightly revised version of Cranmer's Prayer Books of 1549 and 1552. Its prayers and phrases have inspired the worship of the Church of England and its associated Churches for over 300 years. The book enshrines some of the most precious truths of the Bible. Its compilers incorporated in its services something of the spiritual simplicity and directness which is characteristic both of the Church of England and of Christianity itself.

The new Prayer Book intended to make clear that the Anglican Church was an episcopalian one. This it did by changing the words in the Litany 'Bishops, Pastors and Ministers' into 'Bishops, Priests and Deacons' and by the substitution of the word 'Priest' for 'Minister' in the rubric before the Absolution in Morning and Evening Prayer. The 'Black Rubric', deleted from the Book of Common Prayer of 1559, was restored. This was the requirement that all communicants should kneel when receiving Holy Communion. This had been omitted as Protestants considered it to be an acceptance of the Roman Catholic practice of adoration and transubstantiation in the Mass; the 'Black Rubric' explained why communicants should kneel and that, in doing so, they were not accepting Roman Catholic doctrine.

The 1662 revision of the Prayer Book marked the Anglican Church as, not only Protestant and Reformed, but also as Catholic and Apostolic. The essentially Protestant character of the 1552 original book remains and the subsequent revisions have done nothing to modify that character. But the trend of events in the 17th century made it necessary to emphasise that the Church of England traced its ancestry to the days of the Apostles and had in no way departed from ancient teaching. In other words, it was not only Protestant and Reformed, but also Catholic and Apostolic. This claim is enshrined in the Book of Common Prayer of 1662. It marks the development of the Church from the days of the Roman occupation of Britain to modern times and hence is vital to understand.

The 1662 Prayer Book was approved by Parliament and remains the only legally authorised prayer book of the Anglican Church to this day. Until the second half of the 20th century the 1662 Prayer Book, together with the Authorised Version of the Bible, were the two true glories of the Anglican Church, its bedrock and an essential part of this country's national culture. In addition to a complete set of services, it contains the Articles of Religion, the Psalms and a full set of directions for use. Inevitably, over the centuries, certain revisions have become necessary. In 1928 the Prayer Book was revised, to bring it up to date, whilst retaining the integrity of the original. At that time Parliamentary approval was necessary, as the established church had no formal power to change its liturgy. Parliament rejected it, but certain parts of the revised Prayer Book, particularly the marriage service, entered into common use. There are not many women today, I suspect, who wish to vow 'to obey' their husbands as required by the 1662 rite!

AM I A BASTARD?

My father had an uncle called Charlie Andrews who, like all his mother's family, was a Baptist. He had spent his life as a Christian missionary in China. There was nothing wrong, of course, either with his denomination or vocation. But Charlie was a right one! My father nicknamed him 'Chinese Charlie'. My father and mother were married in 1947 using the service in the Book of Common Prayer 1928. Good old Charlie got it into his head that their marriage was illegal since the 1928 book had not been passed by Parliament. My father and mother were, in his eyes, living in sin and so I and my three siblings are illegitimate. So, there you have it. I am a bastard. Many have called me this, but not for being born out of wedlock! Charlie was a twit of course. The legal requirements of a marriage are that the parties should be able to marry one another in law, that they agree to the marriage, that proper banns be read, allowing objections to be raised, if necessary, and that it is conducted by an authorised registrar, either religious or secular, and that it is evidenced by a valid certificate attested to by two witnesses. The form of service is irrelevant, whether it be religious or secular. Charlie never understood this and persisted in his misapprehension to the end of his days. Silly man! He and his wife, Auntie Lilla, died without children. My father and his own parents were their closest relatives. They had great expectations that they would inherit the greater part, if not all, of their estate. They were to be sadly disappointed. It all went to cats' homes and various religious charities. Not a penny did my father and his parents see! It all goes to show that one should 'never hold one's breath'! Perhaps Charlie and Lilla were showing their displeasure at my parents' illicit union. More than likely I should think!

The Book of Common Prayer continued untouched largely until the 1960s when the 'fools' decided to intervene. It was necessary to modernise the liturgy to prevent church numbers falling further to 're-connect' properly with the modern age, they said. It always amazes me that these twerps did not appear to realise that Anglican congregations had been falling away since the beginning of the 19th century. This was due to the failure of the Church of England to react properly to the challenges of the Industrial Revolution. It gave rise to the Methodist, other Non-Conformist Churches and the High Church Tractarian movement in the Church of England itself. This is something I will talk about more fully at a later time. The immediate cause in the 1960s was the rebellion, undoubtedly against what were seen as all establishment practices, including the Church of England, at that particular time. As I write liturgical reform has now proceeded to the Alternative Service Book 1980, which is by no means all bad. I understand that this is an interim measure pending further substantial reform if reform is the right word of course.

THE IMPACT OF COMMON WORSHIP 2000

My father died not long before the publication of Common Worship 2000. It is not a Prayer Book as such, but a total liturgical and other resource for the Church of England. Anything that a person could wish to know about doctrine, worship and even music is there. I do not suppose many people realise this. I may be wrong, but I think that what parish priests present to their congregations today is a fait accompli as to the Order for Holy Communion and other services to be used. Almost certainly the Holy Communion will be Order One in modern English (the equivalent of its predecessors, Rite A and Series 3). It is a fine service, but one can quite legitimately opt for Order Two in traditional language. Effectively this is the old 1662 Holy Communion service, which was loved by so many Anglicans, updating the directions and casting out the dead wood. My father liked Order One in modern English well enough (not as much as 1662 of course) because it was a genuinely new service of merit. Then there is Order One in traditional language, equivalent to Rite B in the ASB 1980 (Series 2 as originally known). My father hated it with a vengeance, since he considered it simply a watered-down version of 1662. Then there is Order Two in contemporary language; effectively 1662 translated into more modern English. Well, I do not slavishly agree with all my father's views, but I do here. All that was really necessary for liturgical reform was the Holy Communion 1662 service in traditional language throwing out all manner of directions, commemorations and prayers which had become obsolete over the passage of time. Order Two does this. Why not a combination of Order One (Modern English) and Order Two (Traditional language) for today's Holy Communion services? My only real criticism of Order One is the excessive choice of eight eucharistic prayers! Just how many could any worshipper want? God truly only knows! This would have provided a simple and straightforward choice which could have been used in tandem. I am afraid this was far too sensible an approach for the Church of England which has decided to go down a much more complicated route. What we have currently is a range of choice gone completely mad, particularly, since individual parishes may now put their own forms of service together.

If you wish to look at Orders One and Two Holy Communion, they are readily available on-line on the Church of England under Common Worship 2000.

I do not say that all aspects of the new services are wrong. But what I do believe strongly is that the great 1662 Prayer Book should still be used on a regular basis. All that was ever really necessary was a new revision of the existing book to cut out the dead wood. I realise the 'fools' have won. 1662, whilst still the only authorised Prayer Book of the Church of England, lies largely dusty, festering and unused at the back of parish churches. It comes out only for early 8.00am

Holy Communion on a Sunday, no doubt to appease a few die-hards. Similarly, for occasional Matins and Evensong services. This will cease altogether when the last old fogeys have died off. And what about church attendances? They have continued to fall, since the whole reform movement started, to about only 50 per cent of what they were then. I am not saying that the reform movement has been responsible for all this further tragic decline. But it has not prevented it at all. I will return to the modern Church at a later time.

The rest of the 17th century and early years of the 18th century

Charles II continued on his so-called 'merry' way throughout his reign. Whilst he was astute enough politically to ensure that he did not suffer the fate of his father, he did nothing to guarantee the succession to the throne. He had no legitimate heirs and he refused to put away his lawful wife in order to do so. That action may well, in itself, have been commendable. But, for such a so-called, wily political operator it proved a disaster. Perhaps Charles did not care what happened after him. He did have a recognised heir, his younger brother, James, Duke of York. James was a dour man prone to perpetual nose bleeds. He was a dreadful politician like his father. His problems were mainly down to the fact that he became a Roman Catholic during the 1670s. His first wife, Anne Hyde, had converted also to Roman Catholicism before her death. The couple had two children, both daughters, Mary and Anne, whose upbringing was supervised by the state, since they were direct heirs to the throne, and they remained Protestants.

James' religion became an increasing problem as his brother's reign progressed. Parliament tried to exclude him from the succession. But James survived and, on his brother's death, in February 1685, he became King James II. There was a Protestant rebellion against him led by Charles II's eldest bastard son, James, Duke of Monmouth, which was put down easily. King James indicated initially that he would do nothing to undermine the position of the Anglican Church. He would practice his own religion privately. The establishment of the realm accepted this, particularly, since James' own heirs were his two Protestant daughters.

But it was not long before James decided to try to lift the restrictions against Roman Catholics being elected to Parliament, holding public office and being commissioned as officers in the armed forces. James tried to pass the matter off as an attempt to alleviate the same restrictions which applied to Protestants outside the Church of England. Thus, he was acting entirely even-handedly, he made out. But James allowed Catholics to occupy the highest offices of the kingdom and received at his court a papal nuncio, the first representative from Rome to London since the reign of Mary I.

James used his so-called prerogative dispensing power to get rid of the restrictions against both Roman Catholics and Protestants holding offices under the Test Acts. The use of this dispensing power was upheld by the courts. In 1688 the king issued the Declaration of Indulgence granting broad religious freedom, by suspending the penal laws, enforcing conformity to the Church of England, and allowing persons to worship in their homes or chapels as they saw fit. It also ended the requirement of affirming religious oaths before gaining employment in government office.

Then seven bishops, led by William Sancroft, the Archbishop of Canterbury, petitioned the king that the Declaration of Indulgence was illegal. They were arrested for seditious libel and imprisoned in the Tower of London.

They were tried quickly and acquitted. Great cheering broke out amongst the king's standing army on Hounslow Heath. It was an ominous warning of what would happen shortly.

I have never understood precisely the nature of James' intentions. Was it simply for political and religious freedom for all persons outside the Church of England or was it for an all-out restoration of the Roman Catholic Church as Mary I had brought about over 100 years before? Whatever his real intentions, he was, like his father, a complete political nincompoop! He should have known that the Anglican political establishment would not permit what he was doing. The final straw was a birth in the royal family, usually an event of great joy. After the death of his first wife, James re-married a Catholic Italian princess called Mary of Modena. They went many years without children and then, towards the end of 1687, she, at long last, became pregnant and she gave birth successfully to a son on 10th June 1688. He was called James Francis Edward Stuart, better known to history as 'The Old Pretender'. This was an absolute disaster for the Anglican establishment. James' heir was no longer his eldest Protestant daughter, Mary, but this new Catholic prince, which gave rise to the prospect of a never-ending line of Catholic kings. Some alleged that the baby had been smuggled into the Queen's bedchamber in a warming-pan!

Now James' daughter, Mary, had married the leading Protestant ruler on the continent, Prince William of Orange, the Stadtholder of the United Provinces of the Netherlands. William himself had Stuart royal blood since his mother, another Mary, had been the eldest daughter of King Charles I. William was the main continental opponent of the mighty Catholic king, Louis XIV, of France. A number of leading English statesmen asked now that William should invade England to save the country from Catholic James.

William accepted their invitation. It is thought now that he would have invaded England, in any event, since, under no circumstances, was he prepared to see France and England allied both against him.

In November 1688 the 'Protestant Wind' blew. William's navy was able to carry his Dutch army to England which was invaded successfully. *This gives lie to the myth that this country has not been invaded since 1066.* He landed at Torbay in Devon. Whilst his forces were outnumbered substantially by those of James support for the king was uncertain to say the least. *James was attacked soon by his famous nose-bleeds, which seemed to bring about some form of nervous breakdown. He fled into exile in France in December never to return at least not to England itself.* He was deemed to have abdicated. William and Mary accepted the crown jointly, but William insisted on having full executive power. These events are known as 'The Glorious Revolution'. The Bill of Rights of 1689 became one of the most important documents in the political history of Britain and, never since, has the monarch held absolute power. The Revolution ended permanently any chance of Catholicism becoming re-established in England. The provisions against Roman Catholics holding public and other office were re-instated fully. Some limited tolerance was granted to Non-conformist Protestants.

The Glorious Revolution excluded all Roman Catholics either from the throne or the succession to the throne. The throne would pass to the Protestant heirs of William and Mary and, if necessary, to those of Mary's younger sister Anne. But no such heirs appeared. The next Protestant descendants were those of the royal House of Hanover. They claimed their descent from Elizabeth, the Protestant daughter of King James I of England, who married Frederick, the Elector Palatinate. Their daughter was Sophia who married Ernest Augustus, the Elector of Hanover. It was to this family that the king and Parliament turned in 1701 to settle the succession to the English throne. Under the Act of Settlement of that year the succession was settled on the Electress Sophia and her heirs, despite the better blood claim of about 50 others of Roman Catholic descent. The last Protestant Stuart monarch, Queen Anne, died in 1714, only a few months after Sophia herself. Anne was succeeded by Sophia's eldest son, Georg, Elector of Hanover, who became King George I of England. It is from this Hanoverian royal family that our current one is descended directly, although it is now called the House of Windsor.

Now the second half of the 17th century had been certainly one of the utmost turbulence, both politically and religiously. On the restoration of the Monarchy in 1660 the Anglican Church was re-established to its previous position, until threatened again by the policies of King James II at the end of the 1680s. When the Glorious Revolution of 1688 took place the Church of England was established permanently under its Supreme Governor, the monarch. The power of the Anglican Church was unchallengeable and it was legally and popularly at its zenith. In 1714 Protestant 'German George' ascended the throne and the position of Crown and the Anglican Church was secured all but forever, or so it seemed.

I think this period can best be remembered by reference to the satirical song, 'The Vicar of Bray', recounting the efforts of the eponymous ecclesiastic to retain his parish despite the changes in religion during the reigns of several English monarchs. The text and the melody are as follows:

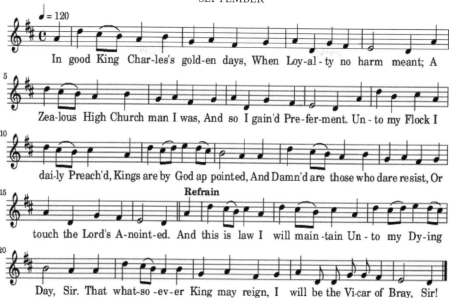

In good King Charles's golden days, When Loyalty no harm meant; A Zealous High Church man I was, And so I gain'd Preferment. Unto my Flock I daily Preach'd, Kings are by God appointed, And Damn'd are those who dare resist, Or touch the Lord's Anointed. **Refrain** And this is law I will maintain Unto my Dying Day, Sir. That whatsoever King may reign, I will be the Vicar of Bray, Sir!

1 In good King Charles's golden days,
  When Loyalty no harm meant;
  A Zealous High Church man I was,
  And so I gain'd Preferment.
  Unto my Flock I daily Preach'd,
  Kings are by God appointed,
  And Damn'd are those who dare resist,
  Or touch the Lord's Anointed.
  And this is law, I will maintain
  Unto my Dying Day, Sir.
  That whatsoever King may reign,
  I will be the Vicar of Bray, Sir!

2 When Royal James possest the crown,
  And popery grew in fashion;
  The Penal Law I shouted down,
  And read the Declaration:
  The Church of Rome I found would fit
  Full well my Constitution,
  And I had been a Jesuit,
  But for the Revolution.
  And this is Law, &c.

3 When William our Deliverer came,
  To heal the Nation's Grievance,
  I turn'd the Cat in Pan again,
  And swore to him Allegiance:
  Old Principles I did revoke,
  Set conscience at a distance,
  Passive Obedience is a Joke,
  A Jest is non-resistance.
  And this is Law, &c.

4 When Royal Anne became our Queen,
  Then Church of England's Glory,
  Another face of things was seen,
  And I became a Tory:
  Occasional Conformists base
  I Damn'd, and Moderation,
  And thought the Church in danger was,
  From such Prevarication.
  And this is Law, &c.

5 When George in Pudding time came o'er,
  And Moderate Men looked big, Sir,
  My Principles I chang'd once more,
  And so became a Whig, Sir.
  And thus Preferment I procur'd,
  From our Faith's great Defender
  And almost every day abjur'd
  The Pope, and the Pretender.
  And this is Law, &c.

6 The Illustrious House of Hanover,
  And Protestant succession,
  To these I lustily will swear,
  Whilst they can keep possession:
  For in my Faith, and Loyalty,
  I never once will faulter,
  But George, my lawful king shall be,
  Except the Times shou'd alter.
  And this is Law, &c.

It gave me great pleasure when I sang this great song at a harvest supper at my last parish in Hatfield Heath, with slightly altered words, I seem to remember, to satirise specifically liturgical reform in the Church of England. I think there were references to Series 2 (subsequently Rite B ASB1980), indeed an abomination before the Lord, and Series 3 (subsequently Rite A ASB1980), which does have some merit, I believe.

OCTOBER

THE 18ᵀᴴ AND 19ᵀᴴ CENTURIES: SOME STAGNATION AND COMPLACENCY BUT SOME POSITIVE SIGNS AS WELL

The Enlightenment

I will mention, firstly, the intellectual movement going on throughout Europe in the 18th century known as the 'Age of the Enlightenment'. Due, largely to scientific advance, many people began, for the first time, to question conventional religious belief, which had been unchallengeable in previous ages. A number of different ideas began to develop during this period about religion. These included both deism and atheism. Deism was the simple belief in God the Creator with no reference to the Bible or any other spiritual source. The Deist relied simply on his personal reason to guide his beliefs. Atheism was discussed widely, but there were few actual proponents at that stage. Rather, people criticised orthodox religious belief but still believed in God as the authority by which evil was punished and, without that authority, society would be undermined. The philosopher, John Locke, said that if there were no God and no divine law, the result would be moral anarchy: every individual 'could have no law but his own will, no end but himself. He would be a god to himself, and the satisfaction of his own will the sole measure and end of all his actions.' Enlightenment scholars wanted to curb the political power of organised religion and thus prevent what were seen as the terrible religious wars that had taken place between Catholics and Protestants in the 17th century.

The 18th century Church of England

The Anglican Church itself responded to these immediate intellectual challenges well, but in the 19th century, it would be thrown off-balance completely by the scientific discoveries of Charles Darwin, which I will discuss later. But, in the 18th century itself, the Church of England decided to adopt an indifferent view to many of the various challenges going on around it. Now that the Protestant succession to the throne and the Church of England had triumphed, the Anglican establishment looked for a much more stable and less politically involved environment in which to operate. The Church of England distanced itself progressively from political affairs other than to line up broadly behind the ruling Whig establishment. This was reflected in the fact that episcopal appointments went to Whigs rather than Tories.

The parish priests themselves became noted members of the local squirearchy. They lived in substantial rectories or vicarages and many became magistrates. The 18th century was the age of Parson James Woodforde who wrote The Diary of a Country Parson, which was not published until the 20th century. Woodforde is often portrayed as someone who spent his life eating and drinking too much, riding to hounds and neglecting his parish duties entirely. This is entirely unfair. What is revealed is someone, who was a member of the gentry classes, but carrying out his parochial duties faithfully. *I could have aspired to this way of life myself; first and foremost, devotion to duty but accompanied by a life of moderate indulgence. This, I think, I would have deserved entirely. I would have had some difficulty in taking part in the hunt since I cannot ride a horse!*

But as the 18th century progressed and reached its end the Church was unable and unwilling to meet the challenges brought about by industrialisation and the vast increase in population that followed in its wake. Even if it had wished to, the organisation of the Church was too out of date to respond. There did not exist dioceses and parishes in the new industrial areas to meet their needs. For example, the Dioceses of Liverpool, Manchester and Newcastle did not come into being until well into the 19th century.

The Evangelical Revival

These fundamental social changes led to a great evangelical revival, both within and outside the Church of England. I will deal with the rise of Methodism shortly. But there was a form of evangelicalism, which took place within the Anglican Church itself, and did not become a separate church like the Methodists. The Anglican evangelicals put great emphasis on conversion, the supremacy of the word of God in the Bible, the preaching of the gospel and the doctrine of justification by faith. They differed from the Methodists over a number of theological issues which I will not go into here. They had found initially that it was difficult to gain preferment in the church, but, by the end of the 18th century, they had been accepted at Oxford and Cambridge and were an established part of the Anglican Low Church tradition.

William Wilberforce (1759-1833) was a member of this evangelical group. He was at the centre of a wealthy group of evangelical laymen known as the 'Clapham Sect'. He co-ordinated also an evangelical group in Parliament known as 'The Saints'. Whilst he is said to have had no party, he was a strong supporter of both Crown and Church, the traditional attributes of Tories at that time. He was a conservative in most of his attitudes. He is remembered now for his great work in bringing about the abolition of the slave trade. His political allegiance is irrelevant clearly, but, since he did such a good thing, he cannot have been a Tory. That would never do for our liberal friends who regard the only good Tories as dead ones! The Earl of Shaftesbury (1801-1885) was a leading evangelical and great social reformer and an undoubted Tory. He was responsible for reforming Factories Act legislation and the abolition of the use of boys as chimney sweeps. *I do not doubt the immense amount of social reform carried out by liberals and socialists. The latter point to the establishment of the National Health Service and the Welfare State. But, again people should grow up and realise that the prerogative of 'good works' does not lie exclusively with one side or the other. Of course, the concept of 'good works' itself is frowned upon by some as exemplifying charity and paternalism rather than universal state provision.*

The rise of Methodism

The major evangelical movement at the end of the 18th century was Methodism. It developed from inside the Church of England. John Wesley (1703-1791), who led the movement, was an ordained Anglican priest. Although the movement led to a separate church after Wesley's death, he himself remained always a member of the Church of England. Wesley introduced unconventional and controversial practices such as open-air preaching, something not approved of by the conventional evangelical Anglicans. Wesley's purpose was to reach factory labourers and the urbanised masses who had moved away from the country to the towns at the start of the Industrial Revolution, towards the end of the 18th century. His preaching centred upon the universality of God's grace for all, the effect of faith on character and the possibility of perfection in love during this life.

The Anglican Church would not accept the methods of Wesley's followers and they were called derisively 'Methodists'. After Wesley's death they ordained their own ministers. Strictly, the Methodist church is a non-conformist church because it does not conform to the rules of the established Church of England.

I think now that the behaviour of the Church of England in not accepting the Methodists was a wholly reprehensible one. It caused a quite needless split. It was the Methodist Church in England which responded largely to the urban challenges thrown down by the Industrial Revolution. The Anglican Church saw what was happening as none of its business and stood by idly. The Anglican and Methodist Churches have no doctrinal differences. The Methodists do not accept the rule of bishops. Inevitably they developed a fine radical tradition, exemplified in the 20th century by Donald Soper, a great socialist. But it remains the case that the two Churches should not have split. I was disappointed particularly in the 1970s when Anglican/Methodist re-union failed over the issue of bishops.*

The development of Methodist liturgy is instructive. In his lifetime John Wesley insisted always on the Book of Common Prayer being used. From the end of the 18th century to the last third of the 19th century all Methodists had to define themselves by reference to the Anglican Prayer Book. Wesleyans themselves saw it as part of their heritage which needed protection. There were other groups in the

---

* Whilst not re-united the two Churches are now in full communion with one another again.

Methodist Church, mainly Non-Wesleyans, who wanted to get rid of the Prayer Book because of, what they saw as, Popish practices. They developed their own prayer books. But from 1936 the Non-Wesleyans came to appreciate the value of the Anglican Book of Common Prayer. The present situation is an interesting compromise whereby Methodist liturgy is influenced by the Anglican Prayer Book. The Methodists published the Book of Offices in 1936, which was influenced heavily by the Wesleyan tradition and thus that of the Book of Common Prayer. The Non-Wesleyans re-discovered their Anglican heritage, even though two orders for the Lord's Supper continue to exist, reflecting both the Wesleyan and Non-Wesleyan tradition. I realise that Methodist liturgy does not stand still. But what a salutary lesson for the current left-wing 'fools' who run today's Anglican Church, where no conservative dares to tread, who have thrown out all that is of value of the Anglican liturgical tradition. These twerps should hang their heads in shame.

The Oxford Movement

For much of the 18th century the old Anglo-Catholic wing of the Church of England ceased to be active. But not long into the 19th century there was a substantial revival in what was called the Oxford Movement. Its original devotees were associated mostly with the University of Oxford. Keble College, founded in 1870, was named after the Anglo-Catholic, John Keble. The Oxford Movement believed that Anglicanism was a direct descendant of the one true Holy Catholic and Apostolic Church; that is, in terms of doctrine, history and practice, it was associated intimately with the Roman Catholic Church itself. The movement's philosophy was known as Tractarianism after its series of publications (1833-1841) called Tracts for the Times. The movement's most famous adherent was John Henry Newman who, together with other prominent Anglo-Catholics, would leave the Church of England later on to join the Roman Catholic Church.

The Oxford movement gave rise to the establishment of Anglican monastic orders for both men and women. Its effect on Church liturgy was profound. The eucharist became more central to worship; vestments became more common and many Roman Catholic practices, such as the use of incense, became part of Anglo-Catholic worship. In mainstream Anglicanism, Anglo-Catholic practice has influenced the usual adornment of the altar with the cross in the middle and two candlesticks at either end on an elaborate altar covering.

Frequently bishops refused to grant livings to Tractarian priests. This led, in part, to some working in the slums where they developed ideas relating to national social policy. This brought the establishment of the Christian Social Union, of which a number of bishops were members, where issues such as a proper wage, a fair system of renting property, infant mortality and industrial conditions were discussed. This wider form of Anglo-Catholicism had a great impact on the Anglican church and its growing communion overseas.

The impact of Darwinism

I think that I have covered broadly the first half of the 19th century, so perhaps now is the time to mention Darwinism. As most of us know Charles Darwin (1809-1882) was an English naturalist who, through his studies, much of which took place in the South Atlantic on his voyage of discovery (1831-1836) aboard the ship, HMS 'Beagle', developed the theory of evolution. Darwin published his findings and theories in his great work, 'On the Origin of Species' in 1859.

It caused a sensation. It seemed to undermine fundamentally the Biblical stories in the Book of Genesis as to the creation of the world and of man and woman in the Garden of Eden together with the stories of Noah's Ark and the Tower of Babel. William Wilberforce had a son called Samuel, who entered the Church of England, and rose to be Bishop of Winchester. Samuel came to be known as 'Soapy Sam' after Benjamin Disraeli described him as 'unctuous, oleaginous, saponaceous'. Thus, he was an oily so and so, if not actually like soap itself. He took part in a famous debate over the legitimacy of evolution with a disciple of Darwin, called Thomas Henry Huxley, at the Oxford University Museum of Natural History in 1860. During the course of the debate Wilberforce asked, whether it was through his grandmother or his grandfather, that Huxley considered himself descended from a monkey. Thomas Huxley is said to have replied that he would not be ashamed to have a monkey for his ancestor, but he would be ashamed to be connected with a man who used his great gifts to obscure the truth. The popular view was and still is that Huxley got the better of the exchange. Many say now that the exchange did not take place. Whatever the case it is so embedded into history that it deserves to be true. *Seriously, Darwin's theories damaged religious belief substantially. Many now cannot take the idea of God seriously, creator or otherwise, given Charles Darwin's discoveries. He did die an unbeliever himself in 1882 and, ironically perhaps, was buried in Westminster Abbey.*

I do not think there is any real incompatibility between the Genesis stories and Darwinism. It is possible entirely to accept Darwin's theory of evolution and, at the same time, to accept also the stories in Genesis. The early Biblical stories are allegorical clearly and express genuine and spiritual truths as to how the world started, the creation of man and how good and evil came about. Whether they are true factually or not is beside the point. Even scientists do not know exactly how the universe began. The good ones will not pretend that they do. There is more chance probably of convergence of views between some scientists and many mainstream Christians than there is between those same Christians and fundamentalist Christian believers who accept the literal truth of every word in the Bible.*

The response of the Anglican Church to some of the challenges of the 19th century.

Whilst the Church of England lost the initiative in responding to industrial and other change at the end of the 18th and beginning of the 19th centuries to the Methodist and other Non-Conformist Churches, it did begin to play a role as the 19th century went on. I have already referred to the great work in reforming factory conditions undertaken by the Earl of Shaftesbury. *The problems caused by drunkenness were addressed by a number of organisations, including the Church of England Total Abstinence Society (1862) not unfortunately an organisation that my son, James, ever joined!*

There were a number of other great Anglican campaigners for social reform. I think Josephine Butler (1828-1906) is interesting particularly. She was certainly a radical rather than a conservative. She is remembered for her campaign to reform the laws relating to prostitution,

---

* I once met two retired hospital consultant doctors, both committed Christians, whose beliefs clearly reflected an almost entirely fundamentalist view of the Bible, whether it be the Creation story itself, Adam and Eve or Noah's Ark.

to secure the vote for women and to reform the laws of marriage under which wives were the virtual chattels of their husbands. She married George Butler, an Anglican divine and schoolmaster, and they had four children, the last of whom died after falling from a banister. This was a turning-point in Josephine's life and she started to address the problems I have mentioned. She campaigned for the rights of women. She became engaged in a long-running campaign for the repeal of the Contagious Disease Acts legislation. These laws tried to stop the spread of venereal disease in military towns by locking up indefinitely prostitutes found to be carrying it. The laws were enforced by compulsory examinations of prostitutes, a process Josephine described as surgical or steel rape. She was successful finally in 1886 when these laws were repealed. She is commemorated today by stained glass windows in Liverpool's Anglican Cathedral and at St Olave's Church in the City of London. A college at Durham University has been named after her. She is regarded by many people as one of the most distinguished social reformers of the 19th century.

Education

In the 19th century the Church of England did play a significant role in education. Before that time there were few schools and, those that did exist, put the stress on religious education itself. Generally, they resisted attempts to provide secular education. In 1811 the Anglican National Society for Promoting the Education of the Poor in the Principles of the Established Church in England and Wales was set up. They founded what were called 'National Schools'. These played a very significant part in the development of education in the 19th century. Whilst most of these schools were absorbed into the state sector by the Education Act of 1944 many, mainly primary schools (about 4,600), still retain their link to the Church of England to this day. The Non-Conformists founded 'British Schools' for the education of the poor. Anglicans and Non-Conformists contributed substantially to the progress of education through Sunday Schools, both before the start of state education in the 2nd half of the 19th century and afterwards.

Other Work

The Anglican Church also spread its wings overseas during the 18th and 19th centuries through missionary work and the establishment of many Anglican/Episcopalian Churches in the Americas, Australasia and other parts of the British Empire, particularly Africa. Whilst this was a very important development, I will not expand on it since my interest lies in the English Church only. But it must be said that that the Episcopal Churches overseas preserve far more of their Anglican heritage than the Church of England itself does today. That, in one sense, says it all.

THE FIRST HALF OF THE 20TH CENTURY: THE WORLD AT WAR

The Church of England entered the 20th century very much as it had done the 18th and 19th before it. It was the established Church of the land, its Supreme Governor was the Monarch and the Archbishops of Canterbury and of York, together with certain other senior bishops, sat in the House of Lords. The Church could not change either the way it was governed or its liturgy except with the consent of Parliament. Whilst the Church had not responded to the new social, intellectual and scientific challenges of the 18th and 19th centuries, as well as it should have done, the majority of people still went to Church on Sundays. Virtually all worshippers had their own Bibles and said family prayers at home. In many households, particularly those of the more 'well to do', family prayers were held before breakfast. The Parish Church remained very much the focal point of community life. This was less so in poorer areas, but it still had some influence.

The opening years of the 20th century were something of a 'Golden Age' in the history of this country, both in terms of national prosperity and imperial power. This was the Edwardian era headed by King Edward VII a man who, after the dour reign of his mother Queen Victoria, brought a much more relaxed and enjoyable atmosphere to the national stage. But it was not long before this atmosphere was shattered totally.

In 1914 a major continental war in Europe broke out, the first since the Napoleonic Wars had ended almost a century before in 1815. Much rubbish is talked about the outbreak of the war in 1914 and the responsibility for this tragedy. Certainly there were a great number who did not see it coming. Today many arrogant people see it as some kind of accident, attributable to the actions of those who did not know what they were doing and whose short-sightedness we have, of course, outgrown today. This was not the case. Imperial Germany was responsible entirely for what happened. It wanted to dominate Central Europe and in 1914 it saw an opportunity to inflict quick defeats on France and Russia to do so. Germany failed and there ensued a protracted war of attrition costing the lives of over 10 million men by the end of the war in 1918. Ironically more people were killed by the Spanish flu epidemic that took place towards the end of and immediately after the war.

Prayers for the dead had been prohibited since the Reformation on the grounds that they implied support for the Roman Catholic doctrine of purgatory. This changed as a result of the First World War. On All Souls Day 1914 Randall Davidson, the Archbishop of Canterbury, spoke positively of the practice. But an authorised prayer for the departed was not issued until 1917. The Low Church wing of the Church of England continued to be opposed. It disagreed with the inclusion of such prayers in the Book of Common Prayer 1928. A final compromise with the Low Church evangelicals on this issue was not reached until 1971 when the terms of a prayer were agreed which could be used ex animo by Anglicans of all theological persuasions. The wording 'asks for such things as we are scripturally persuaded are in accordance with God's will and have not already been granted'. Whilst some conservative evangelicals continue to oppose the practice today the matter is by and large settled.

Needless to say, war and carnage on such a scale undermined the religious belief of many people. How could a loving God allow this to happen? But the First World War was not brought about by God, but by the actions of stupid men. This applies just as much to the Crusades in medieval times and the wars of religion in the 16th and 17th centuries which were carried out purportedly in the name of God. Whilst this subject is controversial inherently, I do not think that there is anything more to say. Many issues are, when boiled down to their essentials, not that difficult to understand.

Only just over 20 years later Europe went to war again in 1939 to stop the German Nazi regime of Adolf Hitler. Many people see this as the only 'Just War' in history, given the atrocities that Hitler was carrying out against the Jews and other minorities. But if Hitler had been prepared to limit his activities to within Germany's own borders it is unlikely that we would have flexed a muscle to stop him. This was the attitude taken then and still taken largely today. What goes on in other countries is their own internal business and outsider countries should not intervene. Britain and France went to war in 1939, just as they had done in 1914, to preserve the balance of power in Europe since Herr Hitler was absorbing busily other European countries. In removing Hitler, which was essential obviously to the war's success, a unique evil was eradicated, one that became more apparent as the war unfolded, to the time that the concentration camps themselves were liberated in 1945.

The Second World War cost the lives of 50 million people, five times as many as the first. It was far more widespread than the first, involving vast numbers of civilian casualties, including 6 million Jews and millions of other persecuted minorities. In fact, when looked at alone, the military casualties of the first world war outweigh those of the second. If you look at any war memorial today the list of names of those killed in the first outweighs by far those of the second. I believe I am right in saying that there were more United States soldiers killed in their one major offensive of the first world war than in the whole of the second put together.

Just like the first the second war did, to a degree, undermine belief in God, but not to the same extent. Perhaps the unique evil of Nazism was something that people understood more than the apparent senseless slaughter of the first war. In both wars National Days of Prayer and Religion and Life Weeks were held, but little permanent good emerged from them. In both World Wars conscription was used. The clergy were granted exemption from compulsory military service since their vocation was deemed to be incompatible with being a soldier. Military chaplains were allowed to serve in the forces and some did bear arms at times. Many were killed whilst on active service. Before going into the Church the future Archbishop of Canterbury, Robert Runcie, was a distinguished tank commander in the second war earning the Military Cross. *On a personal note I spent some of the second war years at Lincoln Theological College. One Sunday we were upbraided by the person giving the address as to why we were sitting comfortably at morning worship in our pews whilst many young men of our age were risking their lives on active service overseas. I have to admit that I was of much more use at home than in the services, given my total lack of athleticism and co-ordination. But I accept that this was beside the point.*

SILENCE IN CLASS

Whilst at Lincoln Theological College my father fell foul of the warden, Dr Eric Abbott, the distinguished future Dean of Westminster. This was for giggling during Bible readings at divine service at passages having a somewhat saucy 'double entendre'. Dr Abbott sent my father down for a couple of terms or so to reflect on his indiscretions. My father would sometimes tell of this, but would not identify the offending references! (So, if you would like to try and identify what they were please do). I do not know how he explained his absence to his austere Victorian parents. On his return to Lincoln my father and Dr Abbott became friends. They exchanged correspondence and Christmas cards throughout their lives until Dr Abbott's death. Dr Abbott was very much my father's theological mentor. (I believe that the late Princess Margaret regarded Dr Abbott as a 'father figure'.) Nothing ever gave my father greater pleasure than when Dr Abbott accepted his invitation to come to Chigwell to preach at evensong. My father had his own small moment of glory when he preached himself at Westminster Abbey.

Whilst this was one of the most momentous periods in world history the Church of England continued in much the same way as it had done before. It had still substantial congregations, but it had nothing much to say about the terrible events going on around it other than 'War is Evil'.

The only real 'change' in Anglican Church practice was the attempted liturgical reform of 1928, a revised and updated edition of the Book of Common Prayer of 1662. Whilst approved by the Church and the House of Lords, full parliamentary approval was not secured as it was rejected by the House of Commons. It was seen, ridiculously, as some form of attack on Protestantism. Nevertheless the 1928 book became widely used, particularly the marriage service, and perhaps much of the problem that arose over liturgical reform in the second half of the 20th century could have been avoided if it had been adopted formally.

THE SECOND HALF OF THE 20TH CENTURY: MY PERSONAL MINISTRY FOLLOWED BY THE 'FOOLS' PARADISE

The period from 1945 is covered by my own parochial ministry. I am going to tell you the story of Church history from that perspective. The main part of my ministry was spent in the wealthy, south-west Essex parish of Chigwell. The history of those years still corresponds with what was going on in the Church of England as a whole at that time. This is I hope, not just self-indulgence on my part, but reflects the trend in most middle-class parishes of that period where the Church of England remained strong at least initially.

I was born in 1921 into a solid middle-class family in Croydon, Surrey. My father was a somewhat austere chartered accountant, originally from the North-East of England. My mother was from a local Baptist family. She died of tuberculosis when I was aged 12. My aunt, my mother's sister, came to live with, and to keep house for, my father and myself. She had lost her own husband in the First World War after only a few weeks of marriage. My father and my aunt married subsequently. It was a sensible arrangement. I was educated at Whitgift School in Croydon. My father had a slight weakness for drink and this caused upset with my step-mother and all her Baptist relatives. I spent many happy holidays, between the wars, on the Isle of Man where my father's sister was married to the Vicar of Douglas. I think that it was his calling that inspired me to become a priest. My aunt and uncle by marriage were a rather naïve pair. They did not have children. I concluded, somewhat naughtily no doubt, that they did not understand the physical side of marriage at all.

On leaving Whitgift I went to King's College, University of London, where I took a degree in theology. It was wartime and the theology faculty was evacuated to Bristol. After graduation I went to Lincoln Theological College where I became friends with the warden, Dr Eric Abbott, the future Dean of both King's College and Westminster Abbey who was my theological mentor throughout much of my life. After the war years I became a deacon and was then ordained priest. I served my ministry in the Diocese of Chelmsford. My parents moved from Croydon to Southend on Sea when their house was doodle-bugged towards the end of the Second World War. I married in 1947 and served curacies in Prittlewell in Southend, Chingford and Saffron Walden. My two eldest children, Mary and Peter, were born about this time. My two younger children, James and Andrew, came much later and I wish sometimes they had not!

I was granted my first living at Great Wakering in Essex in 1952 where I spent two years. The village is in the low-lying area of south Essex and was flooded completely in the great Thames floods of 1953. The only safe place was at the top of the hill where both the church and vicarage were located. The villagers all came up to take refuge. We provided as many of them as we could with refreshments and dry clothes. The clothes were not returned, other than the old-fashioned under-garments, known as combinations, of my mother-in-law who was staying with us at the time. I moved to Chigwell, the major parish of my ministry, in 1954. Now Chigwell was not an area of social deprivation certainly! The 'fools' of today regard such a parish as of no relevance. But I will tell you now the two-part story of my stay, which I think reflects accurately the history of most Church of England middle-class parishes in the third quarter of the 20th century. It was this type of parish that remained vibrant until later decline set in. What the 'fools' forget is that even well-to-do people have souls which need attention, perhaps more so than others in certain cases, where their heads have been turned completely by material wealth.

My parochial ministry in Chigwell

When I became Vicar of Chigwell it was a parish that had seen better days. It needed revitalising. I agreed only to go there myself with my young family when the PCC agreed that a new vicarage should be built to replace the large old, rambling Victorian one which had an all too appealing deep pond for young children to go near. While the new one was being built, in one small part of the large glebe field, the Church provided us with a temporary house in which to live. I think the PCC saw in me just the right type of man for whom they were looking. I was only 33 with a young wife and two small children. I was keen and raring to go.

The church services were the centre of parish life and flourished under my stewardship. The main Sunday morning service was usually Choral Matins with a Sung Eucharist held once a month. We had a strong and accomplished choir to do this. The organist and choirmaster was a small, wiry, professional musician from Yorkshire. He was an extremely capable musician, but he was a highly neurotic man who, despite his unappealing physical appearance, seemed to exercise a magnetic hold on young ladies with whom he developed very close relationships. He had I suppose what is called charisma. He was threatening to resign always, but I kept him on, until, at long last, I could take no more and accepted his resignation. His long-term successor was not quite in the same musical league, but he shared his predecessor's interest in the opposite sex. Such is the way of musicians I suppose.

THE PATH OF TRUE LOVE

During my father's time in Chigwell, Michael, the then Team Vicar, found the organist in a state of some intimacy with a choir lady in the back of his car near the church. Just to cause maximum embarrassment, he banged on the roof to make sure that they were all right. Presumably they had been until this intervention. Michael, whilst a frightful leftie, was always able to puncture the greatest of egos, including my own at times.

Both organists were able to maintain the great Anglican musical tradition, typified by 20th century composers such as Edward Elgar, Ralph Vaughan Williams, Gustav Holst, Charles Villiers Stanford and Benjamin Britten. The music for the canticles for both Matins and Evensong was composed frequently by the people I have just mentioned. These composers and many others also composed great anthems for use at regular church worship. The Sung Eucharist would be accompanied by a special musical composition such as Merbecke. These were great services to the glory of God, using the beautiful traditional Anglican liturgy accompanied by wonderful music. There were also the great hymns of praise with which the entire congregation could join and continue largely to do so now.

Chigwell Church had a large Victorian nave. The main Sunday morning service, held at 11.15am, was, in my heyday, attended by about 100 people. When the service was over the older members of the choir would pop over the road to the hostelry, the Old Coaching Inn 'The King's Head' (the 'Maypole' in Dickens' Barnaby Rudge) where sometimes I would join them. Whilst much less well attended, the other services the 8.00am Holy Communion and the 6.30pm evensong, drew good numbers. I had also a daughter church at St Winifred's, at the Grange Hill end of the parish, and had to fit in a morning service there between the 8.00am Holy Communion and the main St Mary's service. In about 1967 I did have to move the time of evensong forward to 5.30pm, so that we could all get home to watch the BBC Television series 'The Forsyte Saga'! At Christmas, like most other churches, we had a carol service of nine lessons. Both organists ensured that a high standard of music was performed. One of my parishioners went out to the West Indies and enjoyed enormously the candlelit carol services they had there. He suggested that we should try the same thing at Chigwell. So, from the late 1950s or early 1960s onwards we had candlelit services. The tradition began to catch on rapidly all over England. We wondered always whether we had been the first and thus responsible, at least in this country, for this lovely idea. It cannot be proved and may be disproved readily! But that is not really the point. We had a packed church for 'Midnight Mass', which was also candlelit, on Christmas Eve, only disturbed by a few drunks trying to get in from the pub. Similarly, at Easter there was another packed church for the 8.00am Sung Eucharist.

I like to think that I was instrumental in giving new life to all the church organisations. I had a couple of capable churchwardens. I also had two other helpers who I referred to as 'my young men', even though they were not that much younger than myself. One went on to become a churchwarden. John and his wife Audrey were tireless workers for the Church, being involved in the church organisations such as the Men's and Women's Fellowships, Mothers' Union and Young Wives Group. John was a pillar of strength on the PCC. He was always able to give practical advice on maintaining the Church when substantial work needed to be done. He did also sterling work maintaining the churchyard much of it by himself. The other, called Michael, built up a strong and impressive Scout troop, which gave adolescent teenagers something worthwhile to do, and went on regular summer camps. There was also a strong Girl Guides' Group and Cubs and Brownie packs. In addition, there was the usual round of coffee mornings, grand summer fete and the Christmas Bazaar. There was a great fund-raising evening at the vicarage near Christmas time every year where, in contravention of the licensing laws, alcohol was sold! Since I believe that liability for crime endures forever, I suppose that we could all be up before the beak today. But since I suspect that the Grim Reaper intervened for most of us a long time ago, I do not think it is worth worrying unduly. I do not suppose any of this was much different from that which was happening at many other parish churches of that time. *The only source of friction was when young wives refused to join the Mother's Union after they became 40.*

THE NEVER-ENDING DUSTBIN STORY

My own contribution to parish life at this stage was very limited, although as I progressed into adolescence, I was to more than make up for this with various worthless drunken escapades. But, when an infant, I did manage to cause considerable and continuing offence to Audrey and her eldest daughter, Mary, who was about a year younger than me. I was aged 5 and she was 4. At some church coffee morning or other I made an unfortunate outburst in the presence of Mary. I said 'I want to throw Mary in the dustbin'. Audrey looked appalled and young Mary, not surprisingly, was totally upset and started sobbing. This silly story haunted me for the rest of my father's time at Chigwell and still does so from time to time. Both Audrey and the maturing Mary continued to regard me with great suspicion over the years. Not that long ago I happened to mention this story to a close relative. I could hear the almost perceptible sound of disapproval and disdain in her attitude and manner. This did not seem to entirely disappear when I said that what had happened was over 50 years ago and not last week. I apologise now to you, Mary, wholeheartedly, to bring this painful episode (at least for me!) to a final close. After all, both of us became young conservatives. Perhaps we should have married each other. I suspect Mary fortunately missed her chance, married elsewhere, had children and is now enjoying being a grandmother. I do genuinely hope so and I am sure that she has long since forgotten me.

My parochial life was very busy. During the course of my time at Chigwell I had four assistants, three of whom were just curates. The first was a lovely man. I was warned that he was a bit of a 'stage parson'. What that meant was that he rode a bicycle around the parish and loved playing croquet to a standard sufficiently high enough to play in official competitions. *I suspect that croquet is much better as a pastime than as a spectator sport.*

My fourth assistant was somewhat different. By the time the 1970s came the Grange Hill end of the parish had had some housing estates built on it called Limes Farm. *Given a parish of Chigwell's nature they were not too rough.* But I suppose, by that time of my ministry, I did not feel up to dealing with an entirely different type of person. I wanted to recruit someone else to deal with this particular need. The parish was made into a team ministry with myself as Rector with a Vicar to be in charge of St Winifred's and the Grange Hill end of the parish. I recruited a young man called Michael who came with his wife Dawn and their two young children. Some people muttered that they were always 'at it' and sure enough it was not long before a third child appeared. Michael was a good man, but a frightful labourite.

ROAD RAGE

I liked to think myself as a good friend of Michael and Dawn. If truth be told I was already an alcoholic before my family left Chigwell and I was then displaying signs of bi-polar disorder as well. Michael and Dawn put me up because of the untold stress I was causing at home. I do not think Dawn liked it that much or Michael himself if truth be told. We did have wonderful arguments about politics. Years later I did try to renew our friendship, but my continuing bi-polar problems made it all too difficult and I felt it best not to try to keep in touch. My last knowledge of them was when I read in 'The Daily Telegraph' of a vicar advocating verbal retaliatory tactics to people guilty of road rage. There seemed to be no end to the language and tactics the vicar was encouraging Christians to adopt. The vicar was Michael, now retired, who, ironically, had moved to Herefordshire, the same part of the country to which my parents had retired 25 years earlier. Of course, 'The Daily Telegraph' was not exactly Michael's newspaper of choice. But it was mine and I am sure that Dawn must have been terrified that I would try to get in touch! My mood stabilisers only just fended off the urge. Dawn, you can tell 'Land' that 'I told you so'. If you are still out there, I send you my warmest love and best wishes.

Both Michael and Dawn did great work and they were very popular. I was very fond of them both. At the time Michael's sermons were not very good. After my time he moved on to Walthamstow to undertake his ministry in a much more socially demanding area than Chigwell. I am sure he helped to satisfy a great social need. I hope his ministry also had a Christian message as well. Knowing Michael, I am sure it did.

Of course, one of the inevitable concerns of all parish clergymen, particularly those with ancient medieval churches to maintain, is the raising of money. This entails a never-ending round of fund-raising appeals and special events to cover the cost of essential maintenance and other work to the Church Tower, the roof, other external fabric and internal repairs where necessary. One year the whole church organ had to be replaced when thieves stole the lead from over the organ chamber, it then rained and flooded and destroyed the instrument completely. Whilst the cost of the replacement could be met substantially by insurance, my first great organist, *perhaps he was the thief*, wanted a marvellous new replacement necessitating additional uninsured expense. *The same thing happened when arsonists burnt down the church hall. This event reached not just the local, but the national press, involving a picture of 'Yours Truly' standing outside the burnt-out shell saying rather pathetically 'It's ruined'.* The cost of replacement was again met mostly by insurance, but the inevitable desire for improvements, *perhaps the arsonists were various members of the congregation,* meant the raising of extra money. So, there was a constant round of fund-raising appeals to cover the expense of not just these two projects, but all the rest. There were special events plus the usual round of coffee mornings, wine and cheese evenings *etcetera, etcetera.*

Sometimes, I confess that I decided to descend to rather devious means. There were a number of elderly and widowed old men in the parish. They were lonely and waiting basically for the call of the Almighty! They had plenty of money and liked a drink usually. Whilst they did not ever come to church, they liked a visit from the vicar for a good chat. I would arrange to call and we talked happily for quite some time over a drink or two. As far as my host was concerned it became usually a few more than that, so when he was well-oiled, I struck. I told him the church needed money and, surprise, surprise, he would get out his cheque-book and write me a cheque for several hundred pounds, which was a lot of money in those days. *Perhaps I was a bit naughty. But these old boys got a welcome chat and I knew they were able to afford readily the sums they donated. I did not lose too much sleep over it.*

My other parish duties included regular Bible Study and Prayer Groups. But my main parochial work was a never-ending round of parish visiting. I saw it as a fundamental part of my job to visit as many parishioners as I could. I would try to get to know them and their families as well as I was able, and assist with any needs if I could or, more likely, just listen. At that time the Church had a large electoral roll. Every Christmas I would send Christmas cards to each person on the electoral roll and their families and deliver them all by hand. There were a number of nursing homes in the parish which I visited regularly, sometimes taking one or both of my young sons with me, where I would take a service and knock out a couple of hymns on the piano of which I was just about capable of playing. Similarly, I visited hospitals, local or otherwise, not just to visit members of my flock, but also those patients needing spiritual comfort. When people were bereaved I went round to their homes as soon as I could, to give them comfort. Inevitably there were funerals to take most weeks and crematoria to attend. *So, all in all, life was busy even though a number said or would continue to say 'Sunday is your busy day, Vicar'!*

Every year there was a goodly number of mainly young people who put themselves forward for confirmation. Probably, more accurately, it was their parents on their behalf and I knew that the chance of any of these confirmation candidates becoming true Christians and regular Church attenders was remote. But it was always possible that some of the seed sown would germinate. I had a wide choice of bishops to invite to take the confirmation service. In addition to the Diocesan bishop there were three suffragans. *For many years the Bishop of Chelmsford was a man called John Tiarks. If I invited him, I knew what the confirmation sermon would be. It was always under the same three headings 'Come, Do and Go'. When I was asked who was going to confirm the candidates I would, if it was the Diocesan Bishop, say it is 'Come, Do and Go'!* This bishop I did get on with largely, which is more than could be said of his successors. In time I would not invite the

Bishop of Chelmsford to the parish at all. It was always one of the suffragans, particularly the Bishop of Barking, with whom I was then great friends. My snubbing of the Bishop of Chelmsford did not, of course, go unnoticed and when I retired finally in 1986 I was not made a canon, which might have been expected usually for someone who had given 40 years' service to the diocese. *My wife said sometimes that she only married me because she thought I would become a bishop. There was no chance of that.*

St Mary's Chigwell is in a very attractive location near the old Coaching Inn and Chigwell School. It was a very popular place for weddings. They were not usually church-goers, but were attracted simply by the surroundings.*

There were sometimes multiple weddings on a Saturday afternoon. The time-scale could be tight. The couples were warned that they must be on time. Mostly they heeded the warning. Sometimes there might be some slippage, but, since it was the couples' great day, I let them off. *But, on one occasion the bride was getting on for 25 minutes late. I let them know that there was now no time to let them have their chosen music and the sweet words from me wishing them well. All that could be dealt with was a very quick run through of the marriage service itself and the signing of the registers. Served the blighters right!*

I must mention baptisms briefly. In my early days all baptisms were private affairs taking place usually on a Sunday afternoon. I think this is what suited everyone best. In the mid to late 1960s the diocese turned its face against this practice and encouraged baptisms to be held as part of normal Sunday services. I did not welcome this initially, but since I obeyed always what the diocese wanted *(Ha Ha)*, I went along with this. Church congregations were starting to

---

* This was years before castles, stately homes and other attractive places became licensed to hold marriages.

decline and baptism parties, frequently with loudly dressed ladies wearing over-strong perfume, did fill the church. *I came to see myself as a master at dealing with crying children.* On one occasion Geoff Hurst, of World Cup hat-trick fame, came with his wife and family for the baptism of one of their children. In their party was the captain of the England team, Bobby Moore, and a well-known footballer, although not a 1966 team member, called Terry Venables. *Bobby and Terry showed their great respect for the Church by talking to one another non-stop throughout the service. After the service the little boys in the choir rushed down to the main church entrance to obtain the autographs of their heroes.*

Church decline and the 'Fools' Paradise'

So, this was the highpoint of my ministry. A thriving parish church with very strong other organisations to support it. Why did it all go so wrong both for my parish and for others? From the late 1960s congregations began to dwindle alarmingly. It seemed to me at the time that society was undergoing increasing secularisation. Scientific and technological advance went on relentlessly. By the end of the 1960s man had landed on the moon. None of this should have been a threat to religion. Remember what I said about Darwinism. But increasingly people came to believe that there was no point to a God in this wholly rational world where man had the solution to everything. Whilst, nothing new, people came to question more and more why a loving God could allow natural disasters, such as floods and earthquakes, and personal tragedies to occur. Religious belief came to be seen as wholly ridiculous and irrational. The Education Act 1944 (the famous 'Butler' Act) made religious education in schools compulsory. The increasingly secular and politically left-wing educational establishment came to ignore the spirit of the law and made religious instruction simply an exercise in socially good behaviour, not necessarily religiously so. Secondary schools threw out traditional Christian teaching almost entirely.

There was also the thing thrown up by that peculiar decade, the 1960s. There was, of course, 'The Beatles' on whom I did not have a view really one way or another. I do not think they were religious particularly, certainly not in a conventional way: *I think George Harrison came to sing 'My Sweet lord' and John Lennon did come to see himself as some kind of religious guru.* But the real thing that seemed to undermine the established order of the world was the coming of biting satire. For the period of its short run the television programme 'That was the week that was' poked fun mercilessly at the traditional ideas of Church and State, which were the bedrock of the beliefs of myself and other conservatives. That particular programme was just a part of the whole satirical tone of those times which gave people a licence to question the establishment.

A CHOIR'S RIGHT TO CHOOSE?

My father had his own direct brush with the world of satire when, in the early 1960s, the Church Choir chose for its annual outing a trip to see Spike Milligan's 'The Bed-Setting Room'. I was certainly much too young to go myself. But father and others would tell this story from time to time. It is possible that all concerned thought the play had something to do with 'The Goon Show' given Spike Milligan's involvement. In fact, the play is set in London after a nuclear holocaust, something much worried about at the time. It is nothing like the Goon Show.

Many years later I did briefly glimpse the film version myself. I did not watch it the whole way through as it seemed very boring. But I seem to remember, probably inaccurately, people going around in Bishops' mitres and references to homosexuality and abortion, which both were still illegal in the early 1960s. I think you can imagine why a production such as this would considerably upset people of my father's generation, who believed firmly in Crown, Church and conventional morality. But worse was to come. My father and the churchwarden stood to attention for the national anthem and found that 'God save the Queen' itself was mocked as well. The whole thing would not raise an eyebrow by the standards of today. But, needless to say, the Choir was never allowed to choose its outing again. I am sure there followed never-ending trips to such as 'The Sound of Music' and similar!

One of the other major matters was the relaxation of accepted rules of sexual morality. Sex is, as we all know, one of the driving forces of the human condition. One only has to look at the behaviour of kings. King Charles II (1660-1685) springs to mind and, sometimes, even popes and bishops themselves have been guilty of sexually debauched behaviour. In the 19th century there grew up a set of rules known as 'Victorian Middle-Class Morality'. These involved no sexual relations before marriage and absolute marital fidelity. Divorce was almost impossible, certainly for women. Male homosexuality was made illegal. *There is, I think, the wholly apocryphal story that female homosexuality was not made illegal since Queen Victoria did not believe women could do such things.* Abortion was illegal. There was a high level of hypocrisy running through many of these conventions and laws. But, for my generation particularly, they were accepted largely without question. The 1960s turned this all upside down. Sex outside marriage and couples actually living together before marriage 'living in sin' became normal practice. The introduction of the contraceptive pill eliminated largely the risk of unwanted pregnancies. 'No fault' divorce law was established. Both abortion and homosexuality were legalised.

LOVE BEHIND THE GRAVESTONES?

Now, in the early 1970s, my father experienced himself the effects of the permissive society or, rather, the soft-porn film business, whilst he was at Chigwell. One day a film company came by and asked to use the Church for certain scenes. Chigwell School and the Village Shop were also asked for their help. Nobody knew what the film was about and dear father was not the only one not to have asked. The company asked for permission to use a bedroom at the vicarage for members of the cast to change. I seem to recall that my own was used. As it turned out I think more was coming off than going on! The company promised to make a donation to church funds. Work was finished and nothing further was heard. The promised donation never materialised. Months later father was contacted by that great organ for truth and justice called 'The News of the World'. The newspaper had found out that the film was called 'The Love Pill' and involved the purchase of candy at the village shop, containing both aphrodisiac and contraceptive substances. This candy enabled the expression of the love that man has for woman, perhaps behind the gravestones of the churchyard. Like the others concerned my father said that he would not have given his permission if he had known the true nature of the film. The owner of the village shop, a youngish woman, had seen the film and did not see what all the fuss was about. When 'The News of the World' was published the following Sunday there was a headline to the effect that 'Village Vicar shocked by pornographic film outrage'. I think father was more annoyed by the newspaper coverage than the film itself. I googled this great epic of cinema history, not expecting to find anything. But there it was, surprisingly stating that the film had, in fact, been made in the Essex village of Finchingfield, which had been duped into believing it was a serious BBC television documentary. Why there is some doubt for the venue of this great film I do not know. Perhaps the central location was Finchingfield and Chigwell was used for special effects. Who knows? Perhaps both places should engage in battle royal to be recognised as the host for this Oscar-nominated event. But, maybe, they should not fight too hard since 'The Love Pill' receives only a two-star recommendation out of five.

Now, I accept that the changes that happened were by no means all undesirable. The conventional rules against pre-marital sex and 'living in sin' were becoming outmoded increasingly in the modern age. The introduction of 'no fault' divorce was welcome and brought to an end the ridiculous practice of using private detectives to 'ensnare' adulterous couples *in flagrante,* so divorces could be obtained on the grounds of adultery. The legalisation of homosexuality was long overdue. Sexual behaviour is a private matter for individual conscience. Making homosexuality illegal was silly, short-sighted and unenforceable largely, but had still unfortunate legal and other consequences for some.* I consider abortion is a much more difficult issue. The view of the Church is that it is wrong other than in limited circumstances.

The trouble with all this social reform, desirable or otherwise, is that it offended most conventional Church teaching. The Church was seen as 'fuddy-duddy' with nothing to say to a modern audience. This, I believe, was also significant in the decline of congregations. *I have to admit that I was almost certainly a 'fuddy-duddy' myself at that time, but my views have changed somewhat due to the personal experiences of a number of my own children.* Largely none, of what were once contentious moral issues, raise an eyebrow today and nor should it. But, believe it or believe it not, there were days, up and until about the end of the 1960s, when the word 'divorce' was spoken in hushed, disapproving terms.

One of the most reprehensible things that became common in the 1960s and 1970s, among middle-class people particularly, was the practice of wife-swapping parties where those involved exchanged their respective spouses for the purpose of brief sexual encounters. I regret to say that there were a number of my own congregation who took part.

---

* Since my father's death civil partnerships and 'gay' marriage have come about. He might possibly just about have accepted the former, but certainly not, I think, the latter.

This led sometimes to relationships breaking down, divorce taking place and untold of unhappiness being caused to children and others. This was certainly one downside of the 1960s sexual revolution. Whilst people have not gone back to Victorian morality, I think that, by and large, a more sensible and responsible balance has been struck now in the way that people conduct their personal relationships. The worst aspects of the 'permissive society' I think are gone now.

How did the Church react to the falling away of congregations and the secularisation of society as a whole? In order to understand its reaction it is necessary to explain briefly how the Church of England is now run. Soon after the end of the First World War there had come into being the National Assembly of the Church of England in which the laity could participate fully. The National Assembly had the right to send legal measures to Parliament where they would either be enacted or rejected. But, by the Synodical Government Measure 1969, an entirely new form of Church Government came into being by the establishment of the General Synod of the Church of England. This consists of three Houses of Bishops, Clergy and Laity. Below the General Synod there are Diocesan and Deanery Synods. The Church of England has control, mainly through the General Synod, of most of its own affairs. The Laity are elected either directly or indirectly. *Democracy has triumphed and the Church of England is now a wonderful place. But perhaps the words of the American Civil War General, William Sherman, should be remembered 'Vox Populi Vox Humbug'. This means that in large groups of people an abundance of idiots is always present.* But who exercises the actual levers of power is not clear at all. The two senior churchmen are the Archbishops of Canterbury and York. They are both figures who command great respect in the Church of England and the wider Anglican Communion. But they are not chief executives. In practical terms it is likely that executive control is exercised by an informal group of senior bishops, including the two Archbishops, and other senior clerics and laity within the Church of England. *There is a joke that goes 'Who runs the Church of England?' To which the reply is 'No-one seems to know. Ask the organist!'*

The Church of England or, at least its abundance of idiots and 'fools', seemed to think that its problems could be solved by modernisation of the ancient, but still much-loved liturgy. Necessary change should always happen. For those who forget, that is a fine conservative virtue. Now, undoubtedly the Church of England had problems, just as many other churches had, but I do not think that there was any true groundswell of opinion that the services should be 'modernised'. Most loyal remaining Anglicans felt that the traditional 1662 liturgy was of great beauty and value. All that was really necessary was a thorough reform of the existing Book of Common Prayer 1662, such as had been attempted in 1928, to throw out the dead wood in terms of both prayers and rubrics (directions). If this approach had been adopted liturgical reform would have proved a much less contentious and more straightforward exercise. I am prepared to accept now that some genuinely new form of service was justified, probably to be used in conjunction with an old service. That would have been a sensible 'conservative' approach. Ostensibly the Church of England (Worship and Doctrine) Measure 1974 preserves the position of the BCP 1662 as the only authorised form of Anglican worship. But there is nothing compelling its use so it is not used.

A new translation of the New Testament called The New English Bible had been published in 1961. It was a very poor translation and is generally now recognised as such. There have been much better modern translations since. My own favourite is 'The Good News Bible'. Towards the end of the decade the Church of England decided to 'experiment' with liturgical reform itself. What came first were Series 2 and Series 3, both new versions of the Eucharist (Series 1 was the BCP1928). Series 2 was nothing more than a modernised version of 1662 in traditional language which simplified and watered down the old form of service. *I hated it intensely and thought it to be an abomination before the Lord since it was neither an old nor truly modern service.* Series 3 was a modern service genuinely in contemporary language. It had considerable theological and other merit. Why two alternative forms of Holy Communion service could not have been prescribed, giving a choice between a properly revised 1662 and Series 3 is beyond me? That was far too sensible and simple.

A new prayer book called the Alternative Service Book 1980 was published. This did not replace the Book of Common Prayer 1662, but expressed itself to be one that could be used as an alternative. The dreadful Series 2 became Rite B and Series 3 became Rite A. There was also an 'Order following the pattern of Common Prayer' in modern language. So, as far as I was concerned, this was enough. I had not encountered any demand at all for revised marriage, funeral and baptism services. In fairness the changes introduced by the ASB to these services were not substantial. Whilst by no means perfect, I did not think that the ASB was that bad an effort at modern services provided it was seen simply as an alternative to the Book of Common Prayer 1662. But it was made clear that the ASB was only an interim revision before further substantive change occurred.

By now a new brand of clergy was emerging, both bishops and ordinary parish priests, who espoused liberal ideas both ecclesiastically and politically. The traditional view that the Anglican Church was the 'Tory Party at Prayer' had to be removed at all costs. This silly phrase had nothing whatever to do with the modern Conservative Party. The phrase originated in the early 19th century when Tories were identified mostly with supporting Crown and the Established Church. It is a tradition with which I am more than happy to be associated. *That tradition at the time was also said to embrace the sleepy and stupid Tory backbenchers in Parliament. We could do with a few more of those today given the achievements of the so-called live wires.* My own personal views are 'conservative' by which I mean courtesy, politeness and proper respect for others. My son, James, is much more a modern conservative in terms of other matters in which I am not much interested. I think there is nothing wrong with old-fashioned paternalism as such. What does it matter how help for the needy is given, whether it is by way of state provision, charity or purely private donation provided the need is addressed? But true conservatives are now seen as devils with horns and spiked tails. The 'fools' see their ministry, not as the care of souls and spreading the Christian message, but simply that of addressing social need in deprived areas. Of course, this is very important both in itself and as an expression of Christian belief, but it must not supersede the fundamental Christian belief in God and His son, Jesus Christ, as the only means by which eternal life can be obtained. There are umpteen social and charitable workers who do good works with no Christian or other religious belief at all.

So, how is this linked to the liturgy? Quite simply the 'fools' wished to fashion the Church of England in their own image. As part of this, it was necessary to introduce new services and to throw out the old as being worthless. The parochial clergy dictate largely the forms of service to be used. They have swept away progressively the old Book of Common Prayer and have made the use of the new forms of service mandatory effectively. The Church of England today is a place where there is no longer any glory, majesty or reverence in its worship. Whilst I know that I am very old-fashioned surely there are still worshippers who like a service involving a proper liturgy and music. But the grip of the modernists is vice-like now. They will not allow the old Prayer Book for anything other than the Sunday morning 8.00am Holy Communion service, the occasional Matins or Evensong just to please a few old fogeys who will die off shortly. That is the frightening thing. 'The fools' have won hands down because we, the opposition, gave up the fight years ago. Well we never fought at all if truth be told. So, it begs the question who, in fact, were the true 'fools' really?

Despite the total victory of the so-called reformers, Church of England congregations have continued to dwindle alarmingly since this whole process of liturgical reform started in the 1960s. I believe congregations are only about one half of what they were then. I would not be so stupid as to blame this entirely on liturgical reform, but I believe it has had an impact. The attendances of other churches have fallen as well, but not as much as those of the Church of England. I think the other churches, such as the Roman Catholics, despite major changes to their own liturgy, and the Methodists, have remained far more true to their own traditions. I suppose that the 'fools' would say that what is left of Anglicanism is far more vibrant and alive than was the case. But as a truly broad and well-supported national church I fear it is on the road to nowhere. The 'fools' would say also that there is no point trying to restore any of the traditional liturgy because people do not want it. But they have engineered this situation. Most people now have no knowledge of the old liturgy.

By 1978 I'd had enough of being at Chigwell. I had seen what I had built up all fall apart. There were, I knew, some of the younger people who wanted a change. Whether they were 'fools' as well or just wanted a new broom I do not know. Everything about the Church of England that I had been brought up to believe in was under threat. I had still eight years to go before I could retire and the opportunity came to go to a much smaller parish in Essex called Hatfield Heath. There I went until I retired finally in 1986 and went down to Herefordshire for peace and quiet.

FURTHER MARRIAGE LINES

I think you have realised by now that my father could be a very indiscreet man. In his last parish at Hatfield Heath in Essex he caused a row in a good local church family when he read the Banns of Marriage of the daughter of the house. The reading of Banns is a boring exercise to say the least. Nobody says a thing and this story proves that it should have stayed that way. One Sunday morning father decided to inject some life into the reading of the Banns. He encouraged someone to raise an objection. Complete silence of course. But he persisted and, in the end, the daughter's adolescent brother piped up 'Well, she's very bossy'! Probably very accurate. It was only a harmless joke. It was the type of thing that neither my father nor I could resist. Unfortunately, the other members of the daughter's family did not take it this way. They blamed the brother entirely for what had happened. The daughter's mother apologised for her son profusely after the service. Despite my father's protestations that if, it was anybody's fault, it was his, the mother would have none of it. Father thought what was he going to do? This poor young man was being made to suffer grievously for his indiscretion. Slightly later in the day father called round to the family home and assumed total responsibility again. But as far as he could see the young man had been despatched to outer Siberia. I regret to say that the mother refused to let father accept responsibility and I assume the poor young man is still out in the cold somewhere now having reached middle age! Yes, father was stupid, just as I am, in similar situations. But then other people are as stupid, if not more stupid, than us really. Have a sense of humour. Life is too short for this kind of po-faced nonsense!

Unfortunately, my beloved wife Margaret died in 1988, but I was lucky that I was able to remarry a widow lady a few years later. *She had the same Christian name as my first wife so I never got confused.* At that time in the late 1980s and 1990s the small rural parishes of Herefordshire remained untouched largely by the 'fools'. I am able to practice traditional Anglicanism without disturbance. I was christened by my friends the 'Bishop of Bridge Sollars' and we all enjoy ourselves thoroughly by going around the small country churches, where the Book of Common Prayer 1662 reigns supreme still.

Whither the Church of England now? I fear very much that the long-term future is not good. Probably the Church will become disestablished in time because the 'fools' will not be able to see the point in it continuing to be so, and think that it will be better off without its link to the Crown. Once that happens the great Anglican Church will just be one, probably small, religious sect amongst many others. Some traditional Anglicans went over to Rome when, in 1994, the ordination of women was permitted. I have no wish to do this and, for better or for worse, I will die a member of the Anglican Church. But I know that, in the eyes of the 'fools', that is just how they see me; a geriatric fool of use no longer. *Given half the chance I would throttle them all for what they have done. The Church of England is no longer a serious Church for adult people. I have a very low opinion of many of the Archbishops, Bishops and parochial clergy of today. Many of them believe scarcely in God and Jesus Christ at all. The Archbishops of Canterbury of my time were an uninspiring lot really other than dear old Michael Ramsey, a man of true holiness and sanctity, and Robert Runcie who, whilst a social liberal, was a man of clear integrity and courage.*

EPILOGUE

WHERE IN GOD'S NAME DOES THE CHURCH OF ENGLAND GO FROM NOW?

My father died in 1998 over 20 years ago. The Church of England has certainly moved on from then. I am going to tell you certain things my father missed and what seems to be happening now. I am sure the things my father overlooked may well seem very obvious to you, but they are no less relevant for that.

The way life is lived now

One major factor, which my father did not appreciate, in the decline of church congregations in modern times is the fundamental change to the way life is lived now. Until well into the 1960s families largely consisted of a father working regular 9 to 5 type hours and a mother who stayed at home to look after the children and the house. Evenings and weekends were free for family and other activities. This meant that, when a father got home from work in the evening, he had time for a meal with his family, to play with his children and then go out, perhaps to the pub, or to attend a meeting of a local or church organisation. The weekend could be devoted exclusively to both church and family activities. This all began to change radically from the 1960s.

The demands of the workplace became more and more demanding. No longer 9 to 5, but more like 8 to 8 with conferences and trips at weekends sometimes required. Women, either to fulfil their own aspirations or simply to earn more money for the family, began to go out to work themselves. The role of the traditional housewife largely came to an end. The outcome of this was to change fundamentally the whole basis of family life. If parents were now working all hours, childminders and others had to be employed to look after children outside school hours until Mum and Dad got home. There was certainly no time now for parents to go out, either to church or other organisations during the week. This spread into the weekend. People are almost the prisoners of their employers if they wish to fulfil their financial goals and aspirations.

This undoubtedly has had a disastrous effect on the life of both the church and other organisations. People simply do not have the time to take part. What little free time there is must be devoted entirely to their families. Attendances at many non-church organisations like history societies, choral societies, gardening groups and others have become sparse with the membership increasingly elderly. They are only replenished when new members have retired themselves. The particular problem for the church itself is that a whole generation, my own in fact, has now grown up with largely no Christian background at all. They may start attending traditional secular organisations again on retirement, but not the Church itself. They have never been touched by Christianity so they are not going to start now. If they do not see themselves as Christians it is most unlikely that their own children will do so. This continues from generation to generation. I think this change in the way that people live now is a fundamental problem for today's Church

THE PURGING OF THE AUGEAN KENNELS

No story about my father's life would be complete without recalling his interaction with the canine of the species. I have not mentioned this before because I was, and remain, genuinely worried about how most right-thinking people would react. But it is an aspect of his record that must be told. My family always had dogs as pets. As other families do, we loved them all. But father did not realise that, in return for the dog's unswerving loyalty, he had to look after it properly. I believe the first family dog may have been called Sam. He was definitely before my time. His only problem was that he was big. That disqualified him from a long stay with us as no responsible parents could have such a beast among young children! Anyway, he had to go to a new home. As you will discover, from Sam's point of view, this was the best thing that could ever have happened! The first to fall foul of father's lack of care, so I am told, was a lovely cocker spaniel called Sally. She may have been around briefly in my time, when I was a babe in arms, but I do not remember her. In those far off days my father said Matins every weekday morning in Chigwell Church. He did not bring Sally with him but left the door open so that she could come across the busy road to Church a little later, push open the door with her nose and join my father while he said the office. He found this very sweet. Unfortunately, the inevitable happened and Sally was killed crossing the road one morning. Quite some years later a similar thing happened when a mongrel we had, also called Sally, whom I particularly loved, was taken by father for her usual walk. Although he and Sally were only a very short distance from the glebe field, she was not kept on the lead by the road (she was temperamental and had tried to bite a policeman calling at the vicarage on one occasion!). So, when she saw a cyclist, she charged over the busy road and was also killed by an oncoming car as the first Sally had been. I was heart-broken at the time. In between the two Sallys we had all number of other dogs, including two beagles, who were deemed uncontrollable. They destroyed children's toys including one of mine. I cannot remember what it was now, but after a replacement toy went the same way as the first, the offending beagle was got rid of, not at my instigation I assure you. Not long afterwards it was seen with its new owner, perfectly under control of course. After the second Sally there followed Jason, the labrador. His fault was that he growled threateningly when asked to go to bed and had to be prodded into doing so with a billiard cue! Needless to say, he was regarded a dangerous dog and had to be got rid of. I am quite sure he was perfectly happy with his new owner. Lucky Jason, I think! The final straw was in my father's last parish of Hatfield Heath where my sister and her husband presented my parents with a King Charles spaniel puppy called Jamie. Poor Jamie lasted no more than a couple of days before my father took him out and let him wander off the lead near another fairly busy road. You do not have to guess what happened. My mother was so cross that she left father for a few days to visit her sister. Jamie was replaced by another King Charles spaniel called George. He was a genuinely nasty little dog who tried to bite people and chase after sheep. My father could take no action to deal with George whilst my mother was still alive. But after her death and my father's remarriage it was time to strike. How could any reasonable people be expected to cope with such a monster? George was taken to the vet to be sent to Heaven or Hell as appropriate! George was replaced by an entirely soppy and good-natured Labrador-cross called Bess. She was fully protected by my step-mother whose only fault was that she over-fed the dog dreadfully. Otherwise fat Bess was entirely safe and sound I am pleased to say. A family joke had long since developed that, when my father's time came, he would be greeted by a gathering of disapproving dogs who would bar his entrance through the Pearly Gates. Well my father's time came quite some years ago now and I hope God has let him into Heaven even if he has to clean out the Augean kennels every day! My father was no Hercules, so I anticipate this task will take him a very long time. To all dog-lovers this will not be long enough!

Liturgy

At the beginning of the new millennium the Church of England published Common Worship 2000. I do not wish to go over again all that I said previously about the need for a balanced liturgy between Order One Holy Communion in modern English and Order Two in traditional English. Since I came back to the Church at the beginning of the second decade of the 21st century I have encountered hardly any churches which use Order Two as its main service on a Sunday morning, either in the Rochester diocese, where I previously lived, or the much more conservative diocese of Chichester, where I live now. I think that most cathedrals still use the traditional services to a greater or lesser extent. I do get the impression, maybe wrongly, that there still remains some loyalty to the old services in the true socialist heartland of Southwark. It still exists on a reasonably widespread basis for the early Sunday morning 8.00am Holy Communion Service and for occasional Matins and Evensong services, but I am sure this will come to an end once the last remaining die-hards have died off. It is probably easier to go to the local Methodist Church or to visit one of the Episcopalian Churches overseas for a true taste of 1662. Only the English could have brought this truly bizarre situation about. A great and glorious liturgical tradition that came about wholly in this country, but which one now has to go to other churches or countries to hear used! Bloody marvellous as they say. Shakespeare should be banned and come back only as Lamb's Tales.

One truly strange feature of Common Worship 2000 is that parishes are now able to put their own services together, provided certain essential ingredients are included. (Knowing the Church of England nothing will be that essential!) It sounds to me like an 'Ice Cream Parlour' although Common Worship uses a kitchen analogy! When planning 'A Service of the Word' there are, following both the ice-cream and kitchen analogies, three tubs; Preparation, The Liturgy of the Word and Prayers in which are to be placed the different items in the service. There are four different kinds of ingredients and it is important that there is a balance in the way these are used: Word/Prayer/Praise/Action.

Common Worship uses an analogy of a kitchen and a meal. An appetiser at the beginning and coffee at the end. (There is nothing that the Church of England can do today without a cup of coffee, a modern tradition I whole-heartedly endorse!) It is worth noting that for the principal service, on a Sunday, certain ingredients, which are otherwise optional, are required: an authorised confession and absolution, an authorised creed or affirmation of faith, and a sermon. Why a sermon is absolutely necessary, God only knows! Given the standard of some preachers a sermon should be strictly prohibited. In the case of Holy Communion services 'Pick 'n' Mix' also applies. There are basically two parts to the Holy Communion service: the Word and the Sacrament. The Word comprises the first part of the Holy Communion Service; the Gathering and the Liturgy of the Word. The Sacrament is to consist of the following elements: the Peace, Preparation of the Table, the Eucharistic Prayer, Breaking of the Bread, Giving of Communion and the Dismissal. So, there you are, following these rules, a parish may put together its own forms of worship for both eucharistic and non-eucharistic services.

When I first attended my current church, at a small hamlet in East Sussex, the form of Holy Communion service was not familiar. It is a perfectly good form of service, but certainly not Order One or Order Two. I had not appreciated then the ability of churches to put together what they want within certain, not very strict, limitations. (The service used at the church I go to omits in its Order for Holy Communion 'The Peace', *the Holy Huddle*, a so-called essential element, but offending, I think, traditional British reserve!)

The Church of England has been dominated by two major issues since my father's time. The first is the ordination of women and their subsequent consecration as bishops. The second is homosexual clergy particularly bishops. Both issues have caused enormous disquiet and division inside the Church. My father was opposed to the ordination of women. I never discussed the matter with him. I suspect that his objection largely went no further than that Christ and his apostles were all men and that the ordination of women offended the tradition of the Church. Ironically, after his death, one of his granddaughters was ordained an Anglican priest. I am sure he would have been very proud if he had lived to see the day. On homosexuality I never really knew what my father thought. Some think he was a very naïve man and that he would not have known of its incidence in the Anglican priesthood. I am sure this was nonsense and that he knew that many bachelor priests were gay. It was after all perfect cover in a previous age when homosexuality still largely needed to be kept secret. Curiously, there was an exception in the 1970s in the rural Essex parish of Thaxted. The private patron of the living insisted on appointing socialist incumbents despite the almost totally conservative nature of the parish. The patron then appointed a homosexual priest who lived openly with his male partner.

The Ordination of Women

For my own part I never objected to the ordination of women priests at all. I have no doubt their ordination was necessary as the only possible way that the Anglican Church could maintain a full-time priesthood. But that was not the reason for my own approval. When I started going to Church again in about 2011, I was living in the Diocese of Rochester. It seemed that most of the parishes there had female incumbents. My own was no different. This was Seal Chart and Underriver, two hamlets outside Sevenoaks. The vicar was Carol ably assisted by her husband Chris a priest himself, but now retired. I thought that Carol was an admirable vicar. She performed all her parish and parochial duties in a thoroughly professional manner. She could even preach a good sermon. *Well better than Chris. Sorry Chris!* She had previously been a teacher and I think she was a true socialist. I know that Carol has now retired and, should they ever read this, I send both Carol and Chris my warmest best wishes and regards. *I am sure that both Carol and Chris hated my father, not because they had met him, but because they thought I mentioned him too often. Well Carol, he would undoubtedly have liked you and thought that, if there had to be women priests, they should be built in your image. I think that he would have given you the accolade 'Honorary Man'. Don't take it too seriously, Carol. Just laugh!*

My wife and I moved to Sussex in 2015. We live in the Diocese of Chichester. This is as different from Rochester as could possibly be the case. There is not a woman priest to be seen. I do not know how accurate this is, but I am told that the Bishop of Chichester will not ordain women. I understand that at least one of his suffragans will, but women seem to find it exceptionally difficult to find benefices in the diocese after ordination. Apparently, the laity still opposing the ordination of women require some kind of flying bishops for their pastoral care. Well, I don't know about you, but I have never seen a flying pig let alone a flying bishop. Perhaps we should debate which apparition is more likely. Women priests are now well established, other than in my own diocese apparently, and a number of women priests have now been consecrated bishops. The senior Anglican Diocese of London now has a woman bishop. One day, inevitably, there will be a female Archbishop of Canterbury. No doubt she will still not be welcome in Chichester unless decked out as a Boeing 747!

Gay Clergy

The issue of the ordination of homosexual priests and their subsequent consecration as bishops is much more difficult and has been threatening to split the worldwide Anglican Church apart. The conservative African Churches are opposed to the ordination of all homosexuals. The ultra-liberal American Episcopal Church accepts gay priests and has now consecrated some as bishops. How is this conundrum to be dealt with? I have to say that I have really no idea. On a purely secular level I have no problem with this issue whatsoever. Legalisation of homosexual acts between consenting adults was brought into law over 50 years ago now and was long overdue. I have no doubt that homosexuality now should be fully accepted and not just tolerated.

Homosexual acts are supposedly condemned in the Book of Genesis Chs 18 and 19 which sets out the story of Sodom and Gomorrah. In fact, the wording is somewhat ambiguous. Much more clear is St Paul's letter to the Romans Ch 2, where it says that those who refuse to honour God properly, both women and men, are given up to degrading unnatural intercourse, men specifically with men. Presumably women also with women? The ultra-liberals have developed what they see as sound theological reasons why Paul's teaching should not be taken at face value on this issue. The ultra-conservative fundamentalists say the position could not be clearer and homosexuality is to be condemned and certainly not allowed amongst the clergy and bishops. St Paul's teachings on many matters have been controversial. Perhaps his teaching on this issue should simply be ignored. But his writings have been made part of divine scripture, so there is no way that this can be done without some revisiting of the Council of Trent of 382AD where the first Catholic Canon of the New Testament was approved. The possibility of some revision of the Canon is, I suspect, effectively nil.

I really do not know how to reconcile these two positions. I suspect that they are irreconcilable. But there is a perfectly simple practical way for this to be sorted out. The way would be to revert to what was always the position I think, that is the use of discretion. If clergy, including bishops, were just to keep quiet about their sexual leanings I think the whole matter would be easily resolved. At both clergy and episcopal level sexual orientation should remain a private matter. After all this is really no different from the position for all people irrespective of their sexual orientation. I accept that this might rule out civil partnerships and gay marriage for the clergy. A small sacrifice to pay for continued Anglican Church unity I would have thought. All of us in life have to compromise over many things. But the Anglican Communion will not adopt a sensible solution along these lines. It will go on trying to please everybody and end up pleasing nobody.

In a 2017 interview, when asked for his views on gay sex, the Archbishop of Canterbury, Justin Welby, said: 'I am having to struggle to be faithful to the tradition, faithful to the scripture, to understand what the call and will of God is in the 21st century and to respond appropriately with an answer for all people ... that covers both sides of the argument. And I haven't got a good answer, and I am not doing that bit of work as well as I would like'. The Archbishop may not yet have an answer, but some leadership is required. I have advocated discretion. My critics will say this is much too simplistic, but when one cannot see the wood for the trees one sometimes needs a heavy axe to hack through all the extraneous foliage and dead wood to find a way through.

Until 2013 a marriage was a contract at common law based upon a voluntary private agreement by a man and a woman to become husband and wife. Marriage was viewed as the basis of the family unit and vital to the preservation of morals and civilisation. The Marriage (Same Sex Couples) Act 2013 introduced same-sex marriage in England and Wales. To my mind gay marriage is one step too far. I am content to accept civil partnerships as a way of guarding the proper rights of parties to homosexual relationships if those break down. But gay marriage in the Anglican Church should remain illegal. It was never intended that marriage should ever be anything other than a union between a man and a woman. How long will this remain the case? I suspect that the Church of England will legalise gay marriage in due course to keep some of its remaining worshippers or possibly potential worshippers onside.

The whole homosexual issue is now ridiculous. If the wider Anglican Communion does break up over this the fault will lie entirely with the lack of leadership coming from the Church of England itself. The Episcopalian provinces are not subject to the control of the see of Canterbury, but they look to it for guidance. None is coming at the moment. For the Church of England itself the only practical importance of the wider Anglican Communion is that it gives the impression that the Church is still a worldwide one of some significance.

The Renewal and Reform Programme

Rather than trying to re-discover some form of its essential Anglican integrity, I understand that the Church of England is now toying with an extreme form of evangelicalism to revive its fortunes called the 'Renewal and Reform Programme'. This idea has developed from the way of doing things at the Anglican Church of Holy Trinity, Brompton (HTB). There, wholly informal services are held, of an overwhelmingly charismatic nature, where large congregations of sometimes several hundred people speak in tongues and work themselves up into a religious frenzy. This concept has spread to other places and, where religious need is identified, a 'Church Plant' is created. This will usually be in some kind of redundant factory or other large space. Why the term 'Church Plant' has to be used I do not know. Well, I do; the traditional terminology is simply too old-fashioned and, I suppose, is seen as too potentially off-putting to the cool, hip and trendy. Plainly ridiculous. (Whilst I am not a charismatic Christian in any way, I do understand that speaking in tongues, if nothing else, is a perfectly respectable tradition).

Now the appeal is obvious. It appears to bring many much-needed young people into the Church, where overall congregations still decrease alarmingly. Charismatic Christianity in the Church of England is nothing new. It was around in my father's time, although I myself have always associated it with more obviously evangelical churches than the Anglican one. Now if members of the

Church of England wish to worship in this way, they should be entirely free to do so. But I cannot help thinking that this is a further betrayal of the main Anglican tradition. There is neither formal liturgy nor music. It runs totally counter to the old Low Church evangelical tradition itself of the Church of England let alone the Broad Church and Anglo-Catholic ones. Its only seeming merit is to put young bums on seats at least when they are not swirling around in ecstasy! Obviously, the size of congregations is seen as crucial to the survival of the Church. But if, as a result, the Church can no longer be taken seriously what benefit has really been achieved? Surely, the Church of England no longer deserves to be established and it can go off and become some extreme evangelical sect.

Does the Church of England have any future at all?

Clearly the 'Golden Age' of my father's and other middle-class parishes is long gone. Many still try to preserve the traditional round of coffee mornings, annual church fete and bazaar. These are money raising activities to supplement normal Church Services and Bible Study and Prayer Groups. But the Church of England needs a much more modern focus.

Some of this can be found in the vital social work in deprived areas and the charitable activity overseas that the Church undertakes. There are about 33,000 social action projects, from food banks to debt counselling, now run or supported by churches. The vast majority of church congregations take part in such work. Food banks work through the donation of non-perishable food, which is then sent on to suitable community centres for distribution to needy people. This forms the majority of Church of England voluntary aid in this country today.

Additionally, Anglican Churches run or support, to a greater or lesser extent, parent and toddler groups, lunch clubs and occasionally community cafes. Holiday clubs and breakfast clubs, often providing meals to children from low income families, are quite often supported by churches. They can support different kinds of musical events to suit all tastes and ages. Essential English language tuition may be provided to immigrants to enhance their chances of finding responsible jobs. This, I think, fits in very well with my own ideas for reformed church worship and a modern parochial structure for the 21st century which I will outline shortly.

The Christian Church also works tirelessly abroad to relieve poverty and other hardship. There is great work done by Christian Aid, the Children's Society, the Tear Fund and many others. This is an essential part of the Church's mission to eliminate poverty. It follows the teaching of Jesus Christ, who commanded his followers to love their neighbour and look after the poor.

This is all truly praise-worthy work, subject to one absolutely fundamental proviso found in St Matthew Ch22vv37-40 as to the greatest of the commandments:-

37 Jesus replied: 'Love the Lord your God with all your heart and with all your soul and with all your mind.'

38 This is the first and greatest commandment.

39 And the second is like it: 'Love your neighbour as yourself.'

40 All the Law and the Prophets hang on these two commandments.'

First and foremost, belief in and love of God is the true basis of Christianity. Loving your neighbour is fundamental also, but ranks behind the first. Both my father and I, whilst not doubting the essential nature of the second commandment, were suspicious of people using it to claim Christian belief purely on the basis of good works. There are many people who do good things who are both non-Christians and non-believers. It is also true that there are people, who subscribe to belief in God and Jesus Christ and the attainment of eternal life through that belief, who ignore the second great commandment. Both commandments are fundamental, but, without the first, the whole basis of Christian belief fails. Provided that is understood, then the Church's social ministry is an essential part of its ongoing mission in the world today.

I myself have encountered other modern activities such as 'fun-runs' and sponsored 'lose weight' events, neither of which would have appealed either much to my father or myself given our weight and level of unfitness! Most churches have a hall where activities can be held. I believe a few parishes may provide children's creches for working mothers. I have already mentioned parent and toddler groups. Some parishes have Men's breakfasts once a week or month. Similarly, there are Men's Sheds, places where, in the context of doing something practical, the male animal may unburden himself of particular problems to a member of the same sex. This is not something we tough boys find it easy to do. The churches or the halls could and do provide suitable venues for concerts or other musical events. I do not see why these should not be used for plays. Why not T S Eliot's 'Murder in the Cathedral' in the church? If this is thought to be a bit heavy for an average audience, and too demanding for a bunch of amateur players, there are many other lighter and worthwhile works.

Other events could include performances by local bands to attract younger people. The church hall or other venue could become a place where there are pool, snooker and table-tennis facilities. A darts board perhaps. Possibly there could be a licensed bar at such events. I realise this would need close supervision. But most people, certainly unlike myself, do not drink too much too often, even when young. The same thing applies to other youthful activities such as drugs and sex. Drugs are illegal and use on church premises must obviously be forbidden. Sex may not be illegal, but presumably would be participants should be told to go somewhere else (and no, I do not believe there should be condom machines in the church hall toilets!). Whether it be drink, drugs or sex, there will always be difficulties in dealing with young people. That should not stop efforts being made by the church to provide worthwhile entertainment for them. I realise this could all involve great responsibility for the adult people involved. But the Church would be seen to play a direct part in the community once more. This might just provoke some interest in the religious life of the Church. It could provide a basis for a revival of church life, not just in middle class areas, but in less well-off ones as well.

Surely Churches should attempt to maintain an adult approach in relation to both its religious and associated activities. I would advocate a sensible balance of old and new liturgy, maintaining majority use of the new. But there should be room for a traditional Holy Communion service once per month, perhaps with an old-fashioned Matins every fifth Sunday, when there is one, for the main Sunday morning service. Choral services might be beyond the ability of most remaining church choirs now but perhaps area-wide bands of singers could be recruited to perform these, together with a moderately qualified organist, if one is not available at the church. I realise fully that this will not happen without the support of the bishops and the parochial clergy. A support which is simply not there at the moment. Anglicans did not campaign to retain the traditional liturgy 50 years or more ago now, not because they thought it outdated, but because they thought there was nothing they could do to prevent its loss.

What I am seeking is far from being reactionary. It should satisfy a broad range of proper conservative, liberal and socialist opinion. Whilst the Anglican Church has been the worst affected other Churches have seen their numbers decline as well. But the Methodists and Roman Catholics have remained true to their traditions and, if not thriving, are at least not under direct threat to their continued existence in England. To my mind this is the best that the Church of England in the short-term can expect. It may not bring people flooding back through the church doors, but I hope that it would prevent further terminal decline.

I am going to close now with a basic set of services for a normal month in the life of an ordinary parish. I have designed one using a simple mix of the traditional and modern liturgies.

Church of St Lawrence

First Sunday	Second Sunday	Third Sunday	Fourth Sunday	Fifth Sunday
8.00am Holy Communion (Order Two/1662)	**8.00am** Holy Communion (Order Two/1662)	**8.00am** Holy Communion (Order One)	**8.00am** Holy Communion (Order Two/1662)	**8.00am** Holy Communion (Order One)
10.00am Holy Communion (Order One)	**10.00am** Family Service (with or without Baptisms) (Morning Prayer Common Worship 2000 unless other modern service to be used)	**10.00am** Sung Eucharist (Order Two/1662)* *Music (Merbecke) to be led by the St Lawrence Ecclesiastical Church Singers	**10.00am** Holy Communion (Order One)	**10.00am** Choral Matins (1662)* Venite, Te Deum, Benedictus or Jubilate Psalm 23 (The Lord's My Shepherd) Anthem 'The Lions do lack and suffer hunger' *Music to be led by-the-St Lawrence Ecclesiastical Church Singers

It is a perfectly realistic and balanced schedule. The schedule I have prepared still suggests that the modern form of eucharistic service be used most of the time. I am just over 60 years of age now myself and I accept that there are not that many about now who remember regular use of the old liturgy. But it remains a precious resource and, if sufficient support could be rallied, perhaps a successful campaign could be made to restore at least a measure of the traditional services. It might not be easy but if it is successful it will go some way towards the proper restoration of the true Church of England.

If even a small measure of success can be achieved then my father, looking down from Heaven, one or two dogs permitting his admittance of course, might well have a small, gentle smile on his face. Perhaps we can all then rightly say in response to the following invitation:-

With God's Good Grace

The Church of England has been saved indeed

All: **Alleluia**

The Anglican Restoration Campaign

Seeking to promote a balanced old and modern liturgy to restore the true heritage of the Church of England, in which a modern parochial church life for the 21ˢᵗ century may flourish.

Any people interested in supporting this group should email jamesdickinson1921@gmail.com. Should sufficient names be received meetings will be held at suitable venues to set up the group and define its precise objectives and strategy.